the Organic Family cookbook

the Organic Family cookbook

growing, greening, and cooking together

Anni Daulter

SELLERS

PUBLISHING

Published by Sellers Publishing, Inc.

Text and photos © 2011 Anni Daulter
All rights reserved.

Photographs by Alexandra DeFurio
Food styling by Anni Daulter

Sellers Publishing, Inc.
161 John Roberts Road, South Portland, Maine 04106
Visit our Web site: www.sellerspublishing.com • E-mail: rsp@rsvp.com

ISBN 13: 978-1-4162-0638-5
e-ISBN: 978-1-4162-0719-1
Library of Congress Control Number: 2011922575

10 9 8 7 6 5 4 3 2

Printed and bound in China.

Dedication

To my family — as always, you have supported me and loved me through this process. Tim, I love you more than all the stars on a Big Sur night. Zoë, Lotus, Bodhi, and River — you are my heart and soul and my every inspiration. Zoë, you are so creative and an independent thinker and I have come to admire you so much; Lotus, you are the most loving and thoughtful being and your smile lights up every room; Bodhi, you make everyone smile with your silly and warm nature; and River Love, you are the most peace-filled baby I have ever encountered and you teach me about pure joy.

This book is also dedicated to all the families who will enjoy the food and love that fill these pages. May this be our first meeting of many.

Contents

Naturally Tasty Breakfasts

Simple Snacks

Wholesome Lunches

Family Favorite Dinners

Savory Sides

Refreshing Desserts

Homespun Extras

Foreword

There is an old saying, "The family that prays together stays together." I believe that the family that cooks together grows together, and that the family that cooks organically together grows healthy and stays that way together.

I met Anni Daulter when my daughter (now six years old, as this book goes into print) was nine months old. Anni owned Bohemian Baby, a fresh organic baby food company, and she made the most delicious foods for my daughter and lots of babies around Los Angeles. It was one of my first introductions to beautiful wholesome baby food, and Anni and I became friends. We have continued down a similar path of holistic parenting, living, educating, and cooking, and Anni has continued to be an inspiration to me. With my second child, Anni's first book, *Organically Raised*, was my baby food bible. In her second book, *Ice Pop Joy*, she shows us how popsicles can be both nutritious and tasty treats. And now, with *The Organic Family Cookbook*, she takes organic, healthy, and inspired cooking to the next level.

Anni understands how to cook and share a good meal with those she cares about. She knows that at the heart of a healthy family there is a strong relationship to unadulterated ingredients that come straight from the earth, whether it be from your own garden, farmers' market, or natural food store. In this day and age, where disease is the norm, food is truly medicine, and when a parent shows his or her child that the way to good health is through good food, an amazing foundation has been set. Anni understands this and shares it in this book. I have eaten Anni's food, and I can tell you firsthand that it is high vibration food, high energy, and oh so tasty! It is an honor for me to write this foreword on her behalf, and I for one can't wait to go into my kitchen with my family and cook from this book. I hope you do, too.

Anna Getty, founder of Pregnancy Awareness Month,
author, cook, educator, and mother.

Introduction

Cookbooks are a labor of love, and each one has the heart and soul of its author. Right there on the pages is what we believe in, how we cook, what is valuable to us, and why. My first cookbook, *Organically Raised: Conscious Cooking for Babies and Toddlers*, was written from my passion about starting babies and toddlers off on the best possible culinary and nutritional foot possible. With this book, I have been asked to expand this vision to the whole family, so I can share with you how we do what we do. I hope that it helps you find joy and tasty foods in your own kitchen.

I enjoy cooking food that people like — pure and simple — and I want it to be healthy, fresh, and organic. What I have learned about raising a family in a natural way is that a whole lot of time needs to be put into it. Each child has his or her own way to be nurtured and each has something unique to throw into the family soup, so to speak. When we decide to cook fresh, from-scratch foods, it does take some time and thoughtful planning, but when you sit down to that meal cooked with such love and care, it makes it all worth it. The in-between moments with our families — cooking, creating, and being together — make up the goodness of life, and nothing tastes better than that!

I first want to introduce you to my family and myself, so that you feel like a friend of the Daulters by the end of this book. I have four kids and an amazing husband, Tim. I am an eco-minded mama who loves creating in every way, from babies to food to natural crafting. I love every minute of this life and deeply appreciate being given the opportunity to write books that may help make the world a slightly better place to live. I have always been drawn to nature and simple living and have found ways to translate those desires to my family life. I used to be a social worker, but when I found my love for food and cooking, I exchanged my career for a culinary adventure that has taken me down many roads, all of which have unfolded in ways I would have never expected.

My oldest son, Zoë, is 13, a strict vegetarian, and very creative in the kitchen. In fact, he came up with the sautéed banana recipe in the dessert section all on his own, and even helped style the photograph for this book! Zoë was the spark that started me down this culinary path, and he recently told me that he wants to go to the Culinary Institute of America and become a chef one day. When he was born, I did not know much about cooking, but I knew I wanted to feed him fresh natural foods, so I became a mom on a mission. I taught myself how to cook and continued learning at places like Tassajara, a Zen Buddhist retreat, in Carmel Valley, California. It was in those mountain kitchens that I learned the concept and implementation of conscious cooking and mindful eating. I am grateful that these experiences have shaped how I feed my family.

My daughter, Lotus Sunshine, is 6 years old, sweet as an apple pie, and an adventurous eater, not a vegetarian, who actually loves a wide variety of foods. Lotus is a daily reminder of the beauty in every moment. Whether we are in the kitchen cooking or creating natural crafts together, she is always there with a fresh perspective, a creative touch, and a unique spin on the activity. It's exciting to watch her grow into a person filled with the wonder of nature and the true beauty of life.

Bodhi Ocean is my 4-year-old son and pure joy. He is a charmer who loves to make people smile. Bodhi is a particular eater, with a sweet tooth like nobody's business! He loves to bake and mix foods together, like most children, but he is very specific about what ingredients he will use. The other day he wanted to create his own cookies, and asked me for these ingredients: flour, brown sugar, chocolate chunks, pistachios, bananas, and cinnamon. His ability to develop accurate measurements is a little shaky, but he knew what he wanted, and I bet one day he could turn that little 4-year-old's idea into an amazing cookie! I struggle with getting sweet little Bodhi to eat healthy growing foods and have come up with some strategies that I will share with you.

Then there is River Love, the newest addition to the Daulter clan, born in the spring of 2010. The other night at Zoë's 13th birthday dinner, we decided to give River his first taste of food. I peeled and lightly steamed an organic pear, and he gobbled it up. Literally! He was grabbing the spoon and basically yelling for more. He is the last Daulter we plan on bringing into the world, and we are so grateful for his mellow disposition and the ease with which he flows through a day. I aspire to his level of calmness and seemingly astute level of awareness.

The glue of this family unit is my sweet husband, Tim. He is the one who stays up late and cleans our kitchen after long days of food photo shoots, and he carefully tastes everything I create. Among his many talents, Tim is an incredible bread maker. A couple of years ago, we decided to make all our own bread, and Tim took that task on with true baker's hands and heart. He pours the love he has for his family into each loaf of bread he makes, and you can actually taste it! I have included some of his bread recipes in this book for you, and hope they inspire you to start some version of a bread tradition in your own home.

Welcome to my organic family kitchen! I am grateful for my family, as I am sure you are for yours. Pull up a chair at our family table and enjoy the food, friendship, and tidbits of inspiration that will give you ideas on growing, greening, and cooking together with your own family.

In delicious gratitude,

Anni

 # Growing Together

There is something very romantic about going out to your garden, picking a few tomatoes and greens, and tossing them into a salad to enjoy on a warm summer night. It looks pretty and seems helpful to the Earth, and you think it can save you a few bucks on organic produce. While all of this is true, it's also practical, educational, and ultimately, critical.

Today's economy has forced many of us to rethink several aspects of our lives. Now we are more conscious of our everyday habits — how we spend our money and how we spend our time in and out of our homes. For many of us, in times of stress, the impulse is to cut way back; more than ever before, we're determined not to waste dollars or minutes on unnecessary, unhealthy things, including our food. But the truth is, the one place we cannot afford to skimp is our family's nutrition.

The way we grow everything matters! Whether it's vegetables in the ground, apples on a tree, or the milk we drink, it's important to know how these things are grown or processed. We need to know what is going into these products, because they end up inside of us and our children.

When we first planted our garden at home, Bodhi pulled up a chair in front of it and sat down. When I asked him what he was doing, he replied, "I am watching the garden grow. Will it be ready soon?" I thought it was adorable, of course, but I also realized just how valuable it is to begin teaching my children about the process of growing food, where it comes from, how to nurture it, and why it's so good for the Earth and our bodies. Bodhi did not understand the process at all, and I wanted him to develop a natural curiosity and love of food.

I am hopeful that you and your family will want to go "back to basics" and learn how even a simple garden can save you money by producing many of the foods you want to eat. Growing a garden, now matter how large or small, can enrich your children's connection to our planet and help them develop an understanding of where their food comes from. Look for "Growing Together" tips throughout this book to learn more about how easy and important starting a home garden is and how beneficial organic foods are. I also share practical and innovative tips from my family experiences.

Greening Together

We all want to simplify our lives, to not only save our resources, but also to help our fragile ecosystem survive and prosper. I have determined that part of my responsibility in raising my children is to teach them, through our daily routines, how to do their part in "greening up" our home and our local community. By offering you creative solutions that are fun and intended for families, I hope to inspire you to make workable shifts in your family routines and framework.

I love to create new family traditions that, hopefully, my kids will pass down to their families. When it comes to living greener, I think we have to give our children the gift of "eco-understanding" so we have a healthy planet to share with them down the road. Kids can easily be involved in recycling efforts, and are especially great at

repurposing. Lotus doesn't let us throw anything away! Egg cartons become paint cups, crystal holders, fairy beds, rocket ships, or containers for mud pies. Soup cans become flowerpots, and jars get little cozies knitted for them.

Keep an eye out for special eco-family-friendly advice throughout the book called "Greening Together" tips. I'll offer ideas on various ways a family can live a more sustainable eco-friendly lifestyle. Families who make small shifts in their daily routine can make a big impact for the world we all live in.

♡ Cooking Together

The community table is a reference to food beyond what you grow in your own plot. Just as valuable as growing foods for our own family is being educated about food in a broader sense.

My kids and their friends love to cook and help us prepare meals. The more we include them in the process, the more invested they become in their own health. Kids are excited to get involved. They love to help peel potatoes that they just pulled from the garden or toss the salad made with the greens and tomatoes they helped grow. This also ensures families spending more time together, and less time being isolated with life's distractions (think TV, computer, phone). Even young children can help mix in flour for fresh bread or whip honey butter, and these tasty teachings will not only give them practical and valuable life skills, but also will leave them

with loving memories of family cooking days that were spent laughing, creating, and, of course, eating!

What I especially love about cooking with my kids is that I can teach without teaching. For example, just showing them how to shape the bread when we make it from scratch gives them the instruction, without my having to say things like, "Do it like this." The showing is enough. Because cooking with little ones can be hectic and messy, I like to say a little Waldorf verse to bring our focus to the actual practice of what we are doing and away from the chatter of life.

It goes like this:

There once was a wise old bird who lived in an Oak.
The more he heard, the less he spoke.
The less he spoke, the more he heard.
Why can't we all be more like that wise old bird?

A simple verse like this can bring a calm awareness to the kitchen that can then set the stage for
conscious cooking.

Helping our families connect food and the greater
community is also important as we get educated
about the importance of local farming, buying
locally grown foods, and reducing our human
footprint on the Earth.

Throughout the book, I've included "Cooking
Together" tips with ideas about cooking days with family and friends;
reaching out to others by inviting them over for a family meal; helping feed and share food within
the local community; and more.

Naturally Tasty Breakfasts

Good morning! Breakfast gives our day a jump start and gets our blood flowing. Zoë does not like to eat breakfast and would be happy to pop chocolate chip waffles in the toaster every day if we let him. As a teenager, it's critical that his brain wakes up in the morning before school starts, so finding fun and exciting foods for him is the trick to an easy morning transition to the day. Lotus and I prefer savory foods; Bodhi and Tim prefer sweets. Finding solutions to these taste preferences can be challenging, but what is fun about breakfast is that both sweet and savory dishes can be offered, and sometimes a combination of both works very well. In this chapter, I offer delicious breakfast ideas that include a little twist to take them beyond the ordinary.

Pumpkin Pancakes with Honey Butter, Pistachios, and Fig Jam

These pancakes are a fall favorite. I enjoy the spicy flavors and the crunch of the pistachios, and fig jam is good on just about anything. These are great for picky eaters, because they're packed with delicious flavors (as well as healthy goodies!).

Cook's Note: The trick to cooking pancakes well is to flip them as soon as you start to see bubbles forming in the batter. They almost look like little holes on the surface.

2 cups whole wheat pastry flour

¼ teaspoon sea salt

1½ teaspoons ground cinnamon

½ teaspoon ground nutmeg

½ teaspoon ground allspice

½ teaspoon ground ginger

1 tablespoon wheat germ

1 teaspoon baking soda

1½ teaspoons baking powder (recipe page 158)

1 cup buttermilk

½ cup sour cream

1 cup fresh or canned pumpkin purée

1 teaspoon vanilla extract

2 tablespoons raw agave nectar, plus more for topping

2 eggs

unsalted butter, for cooking

½ cup chopped pistachios, for topping

honey butter, for topping (recipe page 150)

2 tablespoons fig jam, for topping (recipe page 151)

Growing Together:
Choosing Plants that Are Fun to Grow

Some things are really fun to watch grow. My kids' favorites by far are pumpkins and beans. They love to have contests to see whose pumpkin grows to be the biggest and whose beans will get to the top of the lattice first. When the pumpkins are ready to harvest, they enjoy carving them, roasting the seeds, and helping me make pumpkin muffins. You can also carve out the inside of the pumpkin and use it as a vase for your fall flowers or as a bowl for your homemade pumpkin soup. Beans are fun to split open and pop right into your mouth.

In a large mixing bowl, combine flour, salt, cinnamon, nutmeg, allspice, ginger, wheat germ, baking soda, and baking powder.

In a separate bowl, combine buttermilk, sour cream, pumpkin purée, vanilla, agave nectar, and eggs.

Add wet ingredients to dry ingredients, and mix until combined.

Melt about 1 tablespoon of butter in a large skillet or griddle over medium-high heat. Ladle pancake batter into skillet to make medium-sized pancakes. As soon as bubbles begin to form on the top side of the batter, flip the pancakes to the second side. Both sides should be lightly browned when done.

Remove pancakes from skillet and keep warm while cooking the remaining pancakes. Serve topped with chopped pistachios, raw agave nectar, honey butter, and fig jam on the side.

Makes 12–15 medium-size pancakes

Garden Breakfast Smoothie and Egg Tortillas

One of my favorite ways to begin the day is with eggs, tortillas, and salsa. When I add a healthy garden smoothie to drink alongside this breakfast, it's the perfect combination. You can also make the smoothie for a filling treat at other times during the day, or turn it into tasty ice pops for an after-school snack.

Garden Smoothie:

2 cups fresh spinach

½ pineapple, skinned, cored, and chopped

1 tablespoon ground flax seed

2 bananas, chopped

2 tablespoons raw agave nectar or honey
  (optional for a sweeter drink)

Egg Tortillas:

½ tablespoon unsalted butter

2 eggs

sea salt and black pepper

2 slices Havarti cheese (or any cheese you prefer)

4 corn tortillas

2 ripe tomatoes, sliced (grab them from your
  garden if you can)

handful fresh basil leaves

fresh salsa, for serving

To make the smoothie, combine all smoothie ingredients in a blender and purée until smooth.

To make the egg tortillas, melt butter in a skillet set over medium heat. Crack each egg into the skillet, but keep separate. Gently crack the yolk, and flip over when the yolk is cooked enough to be sturdy. Season with salt and pepper, and lay a slice of cheese on each egg. When eggs are cooked, remove from skillet and set aside.

Place 1 corn tortilla in skillet, put 1 cooked egg on top with some tomato slices and basil, place an additional corn tortilla on top (think sandwich), and flip.

Flip once or twice until the cheese is fully melted, tomato is softened, and tortillas are browned. Repeat with the remaining tortillas and egg.

Cut in half or in triangles, and serve immediately with fresh salsa.

Serves 3

Bodhi's Warm Berry Quinoa with Honey Butter

Thank goodness Bodhi loves quinoa, to balance out his sweet tooth. This super grain has a nutty flavor and is high in protein. The Incas used to eat this grain as their main staple, calling it the "perfect" food. It's versatile and a nice warm start to the day. For a savory variety, just add a little butter or tamari and sunflower seeds to the quinoa. It makes a great school lunch!

1 cup quinoa (any variety)
2 cups water
honey butter (recipe page 150), for topping
½ cup fresh blueberries, raspberries, or blackberries
1 tablespoon raw agave nectar
½ cup raw pistachios

Put quinoa and water in a pot, cover, and bring to a boil. When it reaches a rolling boil, turn down the heat to low, and cook, covered, for about 10 minutes or until the water has evaporated.

While quinoa is cooking, prepare the honey butter.

As soon as quinoa is done, serve immediately, topping each serving with a small dollop of honey butter, berries, agave nectar, and pistachios.

Serves 4–6

Growing Together:
Go Ahead and Get Dirty

Nobody likes to get dirty more than Bodhi. His pride and joy is getting as muddy as possible, and then telling us about how muddy he is. Gardening is great for toddlers because it's an opportunity to get messy while they learn how to nurture something into existence. When I ask Bodhi to pick certain items for that night's meal, he can't believe his luck that I'm asking him to roll up his sleeves and plunge into the dirt!

Comforting Banana Nut Cinnamon French Toast

This comforting breakfast is a little fancier than what I used to get growing up. Still, it reminds me of being young and chatting with my mom while she made breakfast for my sister and me. Food is a powerful tool that holds many memories, and if we see eating and food as a sacred part of our family life, we will help our children create valuable traditions as they grow into healthy adults.

4 eggs

¼ cup whole milk

1 teaspoon wheat germ

½ teaspoon ground cinnamon

¼ teaspoon ground nutmeg

½ cup finely chopped walnuts

unsalted butter, for cooking

1 loaf brioche bread, thickly sliced

2 firm bananas, sliced

maple agave syrup, for serving

confectioners' sugar, for dusting (optional)

In a large bowl, mix together eggs, milk, wheat germ, cinnamon, nutmeg, and half of the walnuts. Pour into a pie plate or a rimmed dish large enough to accommodate a slice of bread.

Heat a large skillet over medium heat, and add a little butter to melt. Meanwhile, dip slices of brioche into the egg mixture, coating both sides of the bread. Place coated bread slices in the heated skillet. Lay some of the banana slices on top of each slice and press down on the bananas so they do not fall off when you flip the bread. Cook the slices for about 1 minute before flipping, and flip each slice once more until the bread is a nice golden brown color. Keep warm while you cook the remaining slices, or begin serving with maple agave syrup, a light dusting of confectioners' sugar, extra walnuts on top, and a side of banana slices.

Serves 5

Bakery-Worthy Mini Broccoli and Cheese Crustless Quiches

Lotus loves to play "bakery," and these little morning treats are always on her menu. Kids appreciate foods in small containers. The food doesn't seem to intimidate them and appears more manageable and fun.

Cook's Note: I use ramekins for this recipe, but you can use a jumbo muffin pan as well.

1 tablespoon unsalted butter

½ cup chopped yellow onion

2½ cups chopped fresh broccoli

1 teaspoon wheat germ

¼ teaspoon ground black pepper

pinch sea salt

2 teaspoons Bragg's Liquid Aminos, tamari, or low-sodium soy sauce

6 eggs

¼ cup whole milk

¾ cup shredded cheddar cheese

Preheat oven to 350°F. Butter 6 individual ramekins or jumbo muffin cups.

In a large saucepan over medium heat, melt butter, then immediately add onions, stirring occasionally, to start browning. Once the onions are browned, stir in broccoli, wheat germ, pepper, salt, and Bragg's. Cook over medium heat for approximately 8 minutes, until broccoli is softened. Remove from heat.

In a large mixing bowl, combine eggs, milk, and cheese. Stir in broccoli mixture.

Ladle egg-broccoli mixture into prepared ramekins or muffin cups. Bake for 35 minutes or until browned on top. Serve warm.

Serves 6

Blueberry Love Muffins

These muffins are an all-time favorite treat for our family and friends, but I feel that their flavor fluctuates with the freshness of the berries. When blueberries are in season and I pick them from the garden or get them from a local farm, these muffins are phenomenal. When I use frozen blueberries, they are still pretty good, but definitely not the same. So if you can use fresh blueberries here, do it!

3 cups all-purpose unbleached flour

½ tablespoon ground flax seed with blueberries (available at Trader Joe's)

½ teaspoon baking soda

1 tablespoon baking powder (recipe page 158)

8 tablespoons (1 stick) unsalted butter, softened

½ cup honey

½ cup organic raw sugar

2 eggs

1 cup plain Greek yogurt

zest and juice of 1 lemon

1–1½ cups fresh blueberries (decide how "blueberry-ish" you want them to be)

Preheat oven to 350°F. Grease a muffin pan with butter or line with cupcake papers and set aside.

In a large bowl, mix together flour, ground flax seed, baking soda, and baking powder.

In a separate bowl, whip together butter, honey, and sugar. Add eggs, yogurt, and lemon juice and zest.

Mix flour mixture into the wet mixture, a cup at a time, then gently fold in blueberries.

Spoon batter into prepared muffin cups, filling each about half full. Bake muffins for 15–20 minutes or until lightly browned on top. Remove from oven and serve warm.

Makes 12 muffins

Growing Together:
U-Pick Farms

If you want your children to have an experience with harvesting, and you don't want to wait for your own garden to fully grow, try checking out your local U-pick farm. U-pick (or pick your own) farms often offer many opportunities for families to harvest blueberries, apples, pumpkins, strawberries, and many other seasonal picks. The blueberry agave jam I make from blueberry season is heavenly! Check this Web site — www.pickyourown. org — for ideas of farms near you. Before you pack up the family and head out, confirm details about hours and what's in season by checking individual farm Web sites or by phoning ahead.

Mother's Day Sun-dried Tomato–Basil Pesto Ricotta Crepes

Every year on Mother's Day, my hubby and kids bring me breakfast in bed. They make me two kinds of crepes, savory and sweet. I am allowed a few extra minutes in bed and get the royal treatment. My breakfast tray comes with sweet homemade cards, freshly picked lavender from the garden, and these delicious crepes!

Cook's Note: Make the crepe batter first so it can chill while you create the filling.

Crepes:

3 eggs

1 cup whole milk

¼ cup water

1 cup unbleached all-purpose flour or
   whole wheat pastry flour

¼ teaspoon sea salt

3 tablespoons unsalted butter, softened

unsalted butter, for cooking

Filling:

¼ cup oil-marinated sun-dried tomatoes, drained

1½ cups packed fresh basil leaves, chopped

½ cup freshly grated Parmesan cheese

¼ cup pine nuts

2 tablespoons wheat germ

2 large garlic cloves, chopped

sea salt and black pepper

½ cup olive oil

1½ cups ricotta cheese

To make the crepe batter, mix together eggs, milk, water, flour, salt, and 3 tablespoons butter in a blender. Blend until smooth. Cover and refrigerate batter for about an hour, if you have the time, while you prepare the filling.

To prepare the filling, combine sun-dried tomatoes, basil leaves, cheese, pine nuts, wheat germ, and garlic in a food processor. Hit pulse until blended well. Add salt and pepper to taste. Stream in olive oil while the food processor is on low until fully blended together. Blend pesto mixture with ricotta cheese and add more sun-dried tomatoes if you want. Set aside.

To cook the crepes, grease a crepe pan or skillet with butter and set over medium heat. When the pan is hot, pour in enough batter to cover the surface in a thin layer. When the crepe edges start to brown and the middle does not stick when you try to lift it up, use a spatula to gently lift the edges and flip. When the second side is lightly browned, remove crepe from pan and place on a warm plate. Keep covered until all the crepes are made.

Preheat oven to 300°F. Fill each crepe with about 3 tablespoons of the filling mixture, roll up, and place close together in a baking pan. Bake for 12–15 minutes, until warmed through. Serve immediately.

Serves 5

Best Friend Blueberry Dutch Baby Pancakes

My dear friend Tanya turned me on to Dutch baby (German) pancakes many years ago. We would stay the night at her house and eat these light and fluffy treats for breakfast. We'd always have them two ways, sweet and savory. Dutch baby pancakes are very versatile, and you can use any topping you like. For a savory version, just substitute a spicy salsa and pepper for the blueberry topping offered here.

Cook's Note: I like to make these in mini cast-iron shallow pans, but a single large cast-iron skillet works well, too.

3 eggs
¾ cup milk
½ cup unbleached all-purpose flour
1 pinch sea salt
2 tablespoons unsalted butter
1 cup fresh blueberries
¼ cup raw agave nectar
2 tablespoons confectioners' sugar, for topping
juice of ½ lemon, for topping

Preheat oven to 475°F. Place a 10-inch cast-iron skillet or mini pans (6 inches across and 1 inch deep) in the oven to preheat. If you use mini pans, use 4 at a time; this recipe should make about 6 minis.

Whip eggs and milk with a mixer until frothy. Slowly add flour and salt, and mix well.

Remove pans from the oven and reduce oven temperature to 425°F. Place all the butter in the large skillet or divide evenly between mini pans, and swirl to coat pan evenly with the melted butter.

Pour in the batter and quickly put into oven. Cook for about 12–15 minutes, until pancake is puffy and slightly browned. Remove from oven and set aside.

Meanwhile, in a small saucepan over low-medium heat, combine blueberries and agave nectar until warmed and blended, about 3 or 4 minutes.

To serve, scoop warm blueberry mixture onto the center of cooked Dutch babies. Sift some confectioners' sugar on top and squeeze lemon juice over top.

Serves 4 (makes 6 mini pancakes)

Growing Together:
Good Eggs

People often ask me which eggs are the best to buy. I always recommend buying fresh eggs from your local farmers' market, because you can talk directly to the egg farmer about how his hens are fed and housed. Organic farmers typically also support humane living conditions for chickens, such as space for them to roam around and enjoy a natural chicken diet of bugs, seeds, green plants, and more. Studies have shown that eggs from hens raised at pasture have greater nutritional value than those fed non-traditional diets. Growing good eggs means taking care of the chickens and honoring them as special animals that provide us with food we love to eat. Find out where your eggs come from!

On-the-Go 3-Cheese Savory Scones

Scones are a great morning on-the-go food. When we are running late, it's nice to grab a scone on our way out the door. I also like to add one of these scones to the kids' lunches. They are good warm or cold. The trick to soft flaky scones is to handle the dough as little as possible. Be quick and gentle with the dough!

3 cups whole wheat pastry flour

2 tablespoons baking powder (recipe page 158)

1 tablespoon flax seed

8 tablespoons (1 stick) unsalted butter, cold and diced

¾ cup freshly grated Parmesan cheese

4 ounces cream cheese, softened

1 cup grated cheddar cheese

¼ cup chopped scallions

½ cup sliced almonds

1 tablespoon chopped fresh rosemary

2 eggs, plus 1 egg for an egg wash

½ cup buttermilk

½ cup half-and-half

maple syrup, for dipping

Preheat oven to 400°F. If you have a cast-iron skillet, grease and preheat it. If using a baking sheet, grease it and set aside.

In a large mixing bowl, combine flour, baking powder, and flax seed. Mix in cold butter. Add cheeses, scallions, almonds, and rosemary.

In a separate bowl, mix 2 eggs, buttermilk, and half-and-half together.

Add wet ingredients to dry ingredients and mix together to form a smooth dough. If it's sticky, add a little more flour.

Put dough onto a floured surface and press it together for only about a minute, then pat into a 6-inch circle (3 inches thick) and cut into 8–10 wedges. Place wedges directly into warmed cast-iron skillet or the greased baking sheet.

Prepare egg wash by whipping remaining egg in a small bowl. Brush it on tops of scones. Bake for about 20–25 minutes, until golden brown.

Bodhi's Note: Bodhi wants me to tell you all that he likes to dip these in maple syrup. (I have to admit they are pretty good that way!)

Makes 8–10 scones

Growing Together:
Potted Parties

Lotus and Bodhi love to have little parties. We created "Potted Parties," where they invite a couple of friends over to plant some seedlings or herbs in their own personal pots. The children have fun decorating their pots and sometimes even name them. This is a simple way to introduce young children to gardening.

Surprising Baked Buttermilk Donuts

Most folks hear donuts and they immediately think they are bad for you. Truthfully, most donuts are not healthy, but this recipe is tasty, easy, and healthier than most. The kids like to sprinkle the donut holes with cinnamon-sugar for an additional treat.

Cook's Note: When baking donuts, it's easier when you use a donut pan; however, you can use a donut cutter.

½ cup warm buttermilk (not hot because it would kill the yeast)
½ cup warm whole milk (not hot)
1 package active yeast
2 cups unbleached all-purpose flour
2 cups whole wheat pastry flour
1 teaspoon hemp seed powder (use your coffee grinder)
1 teaspoon baking powder (recipe page 158)
¼ teaspoon sea salt
1 cup pure cane sugar
1½ teaspoons freshly ground nutmeg
1½ teaspoons ground cinnamon
2 eggs
2 tablespoons unsalted butter, melted
1 tablespoon vanilla extract
1 cup honey
¾ cup confectioners' sugar

Preheat oven to 425°F and coat donut pan with an organic cooking spray.

In a bowl, combine warm buttermilk and milk with yeast. Let sit for about 5 minutes.

In a large bowl, combine flours, hemp seed powder, baking powder, salt, sugar, nutmeg, and cinnamon. Add this mixture to the milk mixture and stir together.

In a separate bowl, combine eggs, butter, vanilla, and honey. Add to the flour-yeast mixture and whisk together well.

Spoon batter into donut pan, filling each ring ⅔ full. Donuts will rise during baking. Bake in the middle of the oven for about 8–10 minutes, until golden on bottom. You can also bake the donut holes on a separate sheet pan at the same time, until golden brown.

Top the donuts with a light dusting of confectioners' sugar and serve warm. If you make the donut holes as well, coat baked holes with melted butter and dust with cinnamon-sugar (1 part cinnamon to 1 part sugar).

Makes 10–12 donuts

Greening Together:
Valentines

This year we wanted to save a tree and not give out paper Valentines, so my daughter and I made salt-dough heart and star necklaces for her classmates. Lotus painted the dough charms with watercolors and added a little faerie sparkle dust to them. She was very excited to see her friends wearing them all day at school. Salt-dough charms in different shapes make great little gifts for any occasion.

Cinnamon Rolls

Cinnamon rolls are such a warm and comforting Sunday morning treat. This is the recipe that everyone asks us to make when we go for morning visits to our friends' homes. These are a sticky gooey mess of deliciousness. Enjoy!

Dough:

¾ cup warm water

3 teaspoons active dry yeast

4 cups whole wheat pastry flour

1 cup quinoa flour

½ teaspoon sea salt

1 cup whole milk

2 teaspoons vanilla extract

2 eggs

12 tablespoons (1½ sticks) melted butter,
  plus extra for coating dough

Filling:

1 cup light brown sugar

3 tablespoons ground cinnamon

1½ tablespoons flax seed powder

8 tablespoons (1 stick) unsalted butter

1 cup chopped walnuts (optional)

Frosting:

4 ounces cream cheese, softened

1 cup pure cane sugar

2 tablespoons unsalted butter

1 teaspoon vanilla extract

To make the dough, combine yeast and warm water in a bowl and let sit until it gets foamy, about 10 minutes.

In a mixer with your dough hook, combine yeasted water, flours, salt, milk, vanilla, eggs, and butter. Mix until you form a ball of dough. Place dough on a floured or oiled surface, and knead for 8–10 minutes until dough is elastic. Let dough sit in a covered oiled bowl, in a warm place, to rise and double in size, about 35–45 minutes.

To make the filling, combine ingredients in a bowl and blend to a smooth consistency. Set aside.

Preheat the oven to 350°F.

Punch down dough and divide in half. Using half the dough at a time, roll it out on a floured surface into a rectangle, about 12 by 24 inches. Melt a little butter and brush over the dough. Spread half the filling over the dough and roll up like a jelly roll. Pinch seams together with water and flip over to top side of roll. Cut into slices approximately 1½ inches thick. Repeat process with second half of dough.

Lay cut cinnamon rolls, close together or touching each other, in a buttered round baking pan or pie pan. Bake for 15–18 minutes, until golden brown on top.

While rolls are baking, make the frosting. Use a mixer to combine cream cheese, sugar, butter, and vanilla to a smooth consistency. Set aside until rolls are done cooking. Spread frosting on warm rolls immediately after removing them from oven.

Makes 12–15 cinnamon rolls

Simple Snacks

Having children means a never-ending preparation of snacks! It seems like my children are always in need of a snack, and it makes perfect sense: kids' bodies tend to be more in tune with their internal body signals. They inherently seem to know that they need more small meals throughout the day, rather than three big meals. Eating smaller portions frequently gives us more energy when we need it, and the food is easier for our bodies to digest.

I have placed several small kids' tables throughout my house, and each one almost always contains various snacks — nuts, homemade fruit roll-ups, pumpkin seeds, veggie popcorn, fresh fruits, carrot sticks, and cheese and crackers in small bowls. When the kids are walking by, they can just grab a little something to keep their bodies moving through their busy days.

Super Green Crispy Kale

I love this recipe because it's simple, tasty, and healthy. My kids are always ravenous when they get home from school, no matter what, and this super green gives them a megadose of vitamins A, C, and B-12. Serve this with a side of popcorn and you will have a great after-school snack.

1 bunch fresh kale, washed and dried
pinch sea salt and black pepper
pinch lemon zest
juice of ½ lemon
extra-virgin olive oil to drizzle

Preheat oven to 350°F.

Lay kale on baking sheet and sprinkle with salt, pepper, lemon zest, and as much lemon juice as desired. Bake kale for 8–10 minutes to desired texture. Serve warm, drizzled with olive oil.

I like to preserve the leftovers in a glass jar by crumbling them up into small pieces (this will be saltlike in texture), which I then use as a topping on popcorn or pasta. This will keep fresh for up to a week.

Serves 4

Natural Cran-Strawberry Red Roll-ups

Fruit leather and roll-ups are every kid's favorite. It's one of my clever ways to get Bodhi to eat more fruit and even veggie varieties. Consider trying a sweet potato-apple-strawberry combination or even a spinach-pineapple-banana version. What is so great about this recipe is that I can make the purée, save some for River (who is still eating only smooth-textured baby food), and turn the rest into a great snack for the bigger kids.

3 cups fresh cranberries
3 cups hulled and chopped fresh strawberries
juice of ¼ lemon
¼ cup water from steamer pot
2 tablespoons raw agave nectar

Preheat oven to 120°F (or lowest temperature available for your oven). Cover a sheet pan with a piece of heat-resistant plastic wrap or sprayed parchment paper.

In a steamer pot, boil some water. Place cranberries and strawberries in steamer basket and steam for 10 minutes until soft. Remove from heat.

In a blender or food processor, combine steamed fruit with lemon juice and ¼ cup of water from pot. Purée to a smooth texture. (If using for baby food, take out the portion you will need now, before adding agave nectar.) Add agave nectar and blend again.

Pour the purée on the prepared sheet pan in a very thin layer, about ¼ inch thick. Bake, with oven door left slightly ajar, for about 3 hours, until fruit purée has dried. Remove from oven and cut with a pizza cutter into long strips, the full length of the pan. Cut those strips in half, and finish up by rolling them. Store in an airtight glass jar.

Serves 5

Granola Bars

We like to take our kids on nature walks, and what better snack to bring than granola bars? They are a nice balance of sweet and chewy goodness wrapped up in an easy-to-carry bar that even Bodhi can handle with ease.

2 cups whole grain oats
¼ cup sunflower seeds
½ cup dried cranberries or cherries
¼ cup wheat germ
½ cup sliced almonds
2 pinches sea salt
½ cup almond butter
¾ cup honey
1 tablespoon flax oil
¼ cup brown sugar
mini chocolate nibs (optional)

Preheat oven to 350°F. Grease a ceramic or glass 9x13-inch baking dish and line with parchment paper.

Mix oats, sunflower seeds, cranberries, wheat germ, and almonds together in a bowl. Spread mixture on a sheet pan and toast in preheated oven for 8 minutes. Return mixture to large bowl.

In a medium saucepan, combine salt, almond butter, honey, flax oil, brown sugar, and chocolate nibs (if using). Bring to a boil over medium heat and immediately remove from heat. Pour over oats mixture and combine until dry ingredients are evenly coated.

Transfer to the lined baking dish. Press mixture down and together by folding over parchment paper to press down. Tear off edges of parchment paper so it does not cover the mixture when baking. Bake for 25 minutes.

Let cool for up to 2 hours and then cut and serve.

Makes 12 bars

Growing Together:
Healthy Seeds

Seeds are an excellent source of additional fiber, protein, and vitamins in your meals. There is a wide variety of organically grown seeds that you and your family can benefit from. Some are:

Chia seeds: high in fiber, protein, and antioxidants

Hemp seeds: high in protein and fiber

Pumpkin seeds: high in Omega-3 fatty acids and antioxidants

Sesame seeds: calcium, magnesium, iron, and zinc

Sunflower seeds: rich in folate (good for women)

You can read more about them on this Web site: www.globalhealingcenter.com/natural-health/healthy-seeds.

Veggie Parmesan Popcorn

Who doesn't love popcorn? However, many folks have never made homemade popcorn, and do not realize there is a big difference in taste and quality depending on the preparation. Popcorn is a whole grain and contains dietary fiber and protein. This recipe calls for red palm oil, which has high levels of vitamin A and is rich in carotenes. Kids love this snack, and parents can feel good about serving it!

Cook's Note: You will need a large pot with a lid, such as a Dutch oven, or a popcorn maker for popping the corn and (ideally) a coffee grinder to make the mix-in of crispy kale and Parmesan.

5 tablespoons red palm oil

2 tablespoons unsalted butter, plus more (if desired) for finished popcorn

1 cup good-quality popcorn kernels

1 bunch Super Green Crispy Kale (recipe page 46)

¼ cup freshly grated Parmesan cheese

To pop the popcorn on the stovetop, heat oil and melt butter in bottom of large pot on medium heat. As soon as butter is melted, add a few popcorn kernels and wait a few seconds to see if they pop, before adding the rest. Reduce heat to low for about 20 seconds, then return heat to medium. As the popcorn pops, move the pot around over the heat and leave a little air coming in through the top of the pot. When all the kernels have popped (you no longer hear popping), immediately remove the pan from heat and pour the popcorn into a large bowl. To pop the corn in a popcorn maker, follow manufacturer's instructions.

In a small bowl, combine the crispy kale with Parmesan cheese, using your fingers and a spoon to mix well. Or, if you have a coffee grinder, blend the mixture together for about 5 seconds in the grinder. Sprinkle mixture over the popcorn and add optional melted butter to taste.

Serves 4

Parmesan Sesame Seed Twists

The kids love to help make these twists. You might even consider making them for parties. I like to add them to a cheese and olive plate, which makes a great snack for any afternoon. Our favorite cheese varieties to combine with these twists are Gouda and Havarti.

Cook's Note: Arrange cheese, olives, and twists on a nice cutting board or plate to put on the snack table for all to enjoy.

½ cup flour, to roll out pastry

1 package (2 sheets) puff pastry, thawed

I egg, beaten

1 tablespoon unsalted butter, melted

½ cup freshly grated Parmesan cheese

1 tablespoon sesame seeds

½ tablespoon dried dill weed

Preheat oven to 400°F. Line baking sheet with parchment paper.

Roll out puff pastry on a lightly floured surface to a large rectangle about ¼ inch thick. Brush top surface of pastry with egg and melted butter.

In a small bowl, mix together Parmesan cheese, sesame seeds, and dill, then press the mixture into the top of the rolled-out dough. With a pizza cutter, slice long strips of dough, and then twist each one. Place dough twists on prepared baking sheet. Bake for 10–12 minutes, until golden brown. Remove from oven and let cool slightly before serving.

Makes 12–15 sticks

Spicy Lime and Sesame Pumpkin Seeds

The fall brings special treats like fresh pumpkins and those yummy toasted seeds! We NEVER waste the seeds when we prepare our jack-o'-lanterns or make fresh pumpkin goodies. Bodhi loves to put these spiced seeds on his quinoa for breakfast.

about 1½ cups cleaned pumpkin seeds (from a large, fresh pumpkin)
¼ cup sesame seeds
2 pinches cayenne pepper
juice of 1 lime

Preheat oven to 300°F. Line baking sheet with parchment paper.

In a small bowl, mix together cleaned pumpkin seeds, sesame seeds, cayenne pepper, and lime juice.

Spread coated seeds on prepared baking sheet and bake for about 40 minutes or until light brown and evenly toasted. Be sure to stir seeds occasionally. Serve immediately or store in an airtight glass jar for up to 2 weeks.

Serves 5

Cooking Together:
Herbal Tea Stand

I loved having a lemonade stand when I was little girl, and I believe I have passed that along to my kids. We grow mint, lemon verbena, chamomile, and lavender because they make the garden look pretty and they all make great teas. We make a wonderful herbal tea mixture that is infused with fresh lemon and a few shots of agave nectar. In order to brew a nice, gentle tea with homegrown chamomile, for example, take the clean flowers, dry them, and steep them in boiling water for about 12–15 minutes. You may want to add a bit of local honey.

Goodwill Banana Bread

My family likes to bake and give away food to those in need. Every winter holiday, we spend time baking loaves of this bread for the homeless in our city. It's wonderful to see my children putting their loving intentions into creating and distributing this offering. This is a delicious and healthy version of the classic banana bread.

2 cups whole wheat pastry flour

1 teaspoon baking soda

2 teaspoons flax seed

2 teaspoons wheat germ

2 pinches sea salt

½ cup chopped walnuts

8 tablespoons (1 stick) unsalted butter, melted

½ cup raw agave nectar

½ cup pure cane sugar

2 eggs, beaten

4 overripe bananas, mashed

Preheat oven to 350°F. Lightly grease a standard 5 x 9-inch loaf pan.

In a large bowl, combine flour, baking soda, flax seed, wheat germ, salt, and walnuts.

In another bowl, mix together butter, agave nectar, and sugar. Stir in eggs and bananas until blended.

Combine banana mixture into flour mixture and stir just until mixed. Pour batter into greased loaf pan. Bake for about 1 hour, until edges are golden brown and an inserted toothpick in the center comes out clean. Let cool before removing from pan.

Makes 1 loaf

Cooking Together:
Banana Bread Boys

A few winters ago, my husband and sons started "banana bread boys." They gather a bunch of boys and make banana bread for the homeless who live at our nearby Venice Beach. They deliver the bread around the holidays, and the boys end up talking with some of the folks they give the bread to and learning a little bit of their personal stories. This has become a tradition that deepens our connection to our local community and reminds us to live every day in gratitude.

Banana bread is a simple and easy gift to make and share. Make sure to include even your littlest helpers, as they like to be involved in spreading goodwill and making a banana flour-filled mess.

Cooking Together:
Flour Flour Everywhere

Lotus and I were baking recently, when she put her hand in the flour jar and said, "Mommy, I love flour so much, I wish I could play with it all day. It's so soft, it feels like silk." We do so much baking and cooking in this house that it seems like flour is always everywhere. Bodhi is our official baker and mess maker and loves to be in the middle of all the baking that goes on. Flour is one of his favorite things to play with.

Flour is the result of ground-up grains grown from wheat, quinoa, almonds, and others. Here is a quick guide to several different flours, so you might have a better idea of what you are buying.

All-purpose Flour (I prefer unbleached): This is the most popular type of flour and is used in many recipes. Made up of wheat flour and malted (sprouted and dried) barley flour, this is excellent for most types of baking and pasta.

Whole Wheat Pastry Flour: I love this! It is produced from soft wheat and has a fine texture and a high starch content. Because of the presence of some of the bran and germ, pastry items made with whole wheat pastry flour are more nutritious.

Spelt Flour: This flour is like wheat flour, but it has a nuttier flavor, more protein, and is easier to digest. It does contain gluten, so it is not appropriate for folks allergic to gluten. Although spelt flour can be used in most recipes calling for wheat flour and is good for baking hearty items like breads, cakes, cookies, muffins, or pasta, it does not rise as well as other flours and creates a denser texture in baked goods.

Quinoa Flour: Quinoa grain, which is high in protein, produces a light delicate flour great for baking, although it can make cakes somewhat dense.

Semolina Flour: This is mostly used for making pasta and is high in gluten.

Gluten-free Flour: Folks who have gluten intolerance need gluten-free flour. Luckily, several companies now make an all-purpose gluten-free flour that can be used for baking and cooking. It is usually made from some combination of white rice and whole grain (brown) rice flours, tapioca starch, and potato starch.

Rice Flour: Rice flour is lighter and usually easier to digest than wheat flour and can be tolerated by folks who are gluten-intolerant. It's often used to make noodles and sweets and can be used as a thickener.

Oat Flour: This flour is made from whole grain ground oats and contains no gluten. The lack of gluten makes it difficult to substitute in place of other flours when baking, because the dough will not rise if made with only oat flour. Use in combination with a flour with the ability to rise.

Spicy Parmesan Crisps

These crisps make a great snack for after school or a nice pre-dinner-party snack.

1 cup whole wheat pastry flour

1½ teaspoons poppy seeds

½ teaspoon cayenne pepper

1 cup shredded mild cheddar cheese

1 cup freshly grated Parmesan cheese

8 tablespoons (1 stick) unsalted butter, softened

In a medium mixing bowl, mix together flour, poppy seeds, and cayenne pepper. Add cheese and softened butter and mix until it forms a dough. Transfer to a sheet of waxed paper and roll tightly into a log. Chill for at least 1 hour until it firms up.

Preheat oven to 400°F. Line a cookie sheet with parchment paper. Slice the log into ¼-inch-thick rounds and place on prepared cookie sheet. Bake for about 15 minutes or until golden brown. Serve warm or at room temperature.

Makes 20–25 crisps

Heart-Shaped Lotus Pretzels

Warm heart-shaped pretzels out of the oven with pink salt! It's the perfect girly treat (although boys enjoy them too, of course), and they are surprisingly easy to make. These were inspired by a trip to Trader Joe's, when Lotus found the pink salt in the spice aisle and said we should make pretzels with it. These comforting snacks are dedicated to her vision, and they are delicious!

3 teaspoons active dry yeast
4 cups warm water
5 cups unbleached all-purpose flour
½ cup raw agave nectar
1 tablespoon unsalted butter, softened
1 teaspoon sea salt
½ cup baking soda
4 cups hot water (from your tap, not boiling)
pink and white sea salt, for topping

In a large bowl, dissolve yeast in warm water for about 8–10 minutes.

Mix in flour, 1 cup at a time. Then add agave nectar, butter, and salt. Mix dough into a ball, place in a lightly oiled bowl, cover, and set in a warm place to rise for about 45 minutes.

While dough is rising, combine baking soda and hot water in a separate bowl, stirring to dissolve the baking soda. Let cool to room temperature.

Preheat oven to 450°F. Line a baking sheet with parchment paper.

After dough has doubled in size, place it on a lightly floured surface. Cut into about 10 or 12 pieces. Roll out each piece of dough into a long snake shape, and then form into a heart shape.

Dip the heart-shaped pretzels in the baking soda mixture, place on the prepared baking sheet, and sprinkle with desired amount of pink and white sea salt. Bake for approximately 8–10 minutes, until golden brown. Remove from oven and cool before serving. They can be stored in an airtight container for up to 2 days.

Makes 10–12 pretzels

Wholesome Lunches

Making school lunches for three kids every morning is always a challenge, but I am dedicated to making my children home-cooked foods that will give them the energy they need to play and learn throughout the day. Even on non-school days, making hearty lunches is a valuable effort. When your children have lunch with you, consider making it just as special as other meals by allowing them to set the table with real plates (no plastic or paper), cloth napkins, and a lighted candle. We light a candle at every meal, even breakfast, and say a little blessing just to bring some gratitude and focus to our meal together. The children love having the candle lit during meals, as it brings a real warmth to our table.

Piquanté Pepper and Sweet Potato Flatbread

Leftovers inspired this flatbread recipe! I had River's one-day-old sweet potato purée in the fridge and leftover Peppadew peppers (a type of sweet piquanté pepper) from a pizza party we had hosted the weekend before. (If you have never tried these peppers, they are AMAZING! The perfect blend of sweet and spicy. You can buy them in your local natural food stores at the olive bar or in jars from the Peppadew brand.) Flatbreads (available at almost any grocery store) are great for a quick and easy lunch, as you can easily custom-make them for various culinary preferences and on-hand ingredients and leftovers.

Cook's Note: Whether I am making a pizza or a flatbread, I always heat up the dough or flatbread prior to cooking. This makes the crust deliciously crispy.

1 medium sweet potato
1 large piece flatbread
½ cup sliced red onions
olive oil
½ cup grated mozzarella cheese
½ cup crumbled feta cheese
handful chopped sweet piquanté peppers
pinch dried oregano

Peel sweet potato and cut into large chunks. Put chunks in a steamer over simmering water and steam until softened, about 12 minutes. Transfer steamed pieces to a blender and purée. (If you have a baby, save some for a healthy fresh meal.) Set aside.

Preheat oven to 425°F.

On a pizza stone or a cookie sheet, place flatbread in the oven without any of the toppings, for 5 minutes.

Meanwhile, sauté onions in a skillet with a little olive oil over medium heat until caramelized and softened, about 5–7 minutes.

Remove flatbread from oven and spread sweet potato purée over the top. Sprinkle with both cheeses, onions, peppers, and oregano, then drizzle all over with a touch of olive oil.

Bake flatbread for 10–12 more minutes, until cheeses are melted and slightly browned. Serve hot.

Serves 2

Growing Together: Dr. Greene's Expert Opinion on Organics

Dr. Greene is a highly respected pediatrician and author of *Raising Baby Green* and *Feeding Baby Green*. I asked him why, from a pediatrician's standpoint, it is important for families to eat fresh, organic foods whenever possible. Here is his response:

Children are built out of food. From the sparkle in their eyes to the bruises on their shins, the stuff of their bodies is assembled, fueled, and repaired from food. The food we share as families is central to good health.

As a pediatrician, when I consider all of the health issues in children that have been rapidly increasing in recent decades — problems such as ADHD, allergies, asthma, autism, celiac disease, diabetes, early puberty, high blood pressure, high cholesterol, learning disabilities, and obesity — in each case, the increase is linked to changes in lifestyle and the environment, such as how kids move, how they eat, and what exposures they have. And in each case there is a direct link to food.

This is good news. It means that for our most pressing health issues there are lifestyle and environmental solutions. And in particular, there are food solutions.

Choose clean real food, made without unnecessary antibiotics, hormones, genetic modification, toxic synthetic pesticides, artificial colors, or other questionable ingredients. Food grown on rich, living soil, bursting with complex nutrients and flavors.

In short, enjoying fresh organic food is foundational to a family's health.

Bon appétit!

Alan Greene, MD, FAAP

Refreshing Fall Persimmon Pomegranate Salad

Persimmons and pomegranates are lovely fall fruits that are high in antioxidants and vitamins and are great for digestive problems. Having children means lots of little ailments, so boosting their immune systems with foods rich with vitamins is essential.

Cook's Note: Persimmons also make a warm and comforting tea that soothes an upset tummy. Just boil 4 or 5 chopped persimmons and a little fresh mint in about 4 cups of water and let steep for 20–25 minutes.

5 persimmons, peeled and diced
1 cup pomegranate seeds
2 Gala apples, chopped, peel left on
1 cup finely chopped fresh mint
raspberry vinaigrette (optional; your favorite brand or prepare your own)

In a big bowl, combine persimmons, pomegranate seeds, and apples. Serve with fresh mint leaves and a light touch of raspberry vinaigrette, if using.

Serves 6

Austin and Cameron's Pastrami Bleu Cheese Melt

My nephew Austin loves pastrami and my niece Cameron loves bleu cheese, so together they inspired this recipe. I thought this sandwich would be a great combination that would satisfy both of them. Bleu cheese is a unique flavor that can take some tries to acclimate a child's palate to, so try a little bit at a time and see how it goes.

olive oil
½ cup chopped yellow onions
¼ cup sliced mushrooms
fresh bread rolls, enough for 2 sandwiches
pastrami slices
¼ cup crumbled bleu cheese

Pour a little olive oil in a sauté pan, and over low-medium heat, slowly sauté onions and mushrooms until they are soft and somewhat caramelized.

Slice rolls and assemble sandwiches by layering pastrami slices, bleu cheese, and cooked onions and mushrooms. Place sandwiches in a hot cast-iron grill pan with a cast-iron lid press on top or use a panini pan. Let bleu cheese melt and allow the bread to get crispy. Serve warm.

Makes 2 sandwiches

Cantaloupe and Arugula Salad with Crispy Prosciutto and Spicy Orange Vinaigrette

This is the perfect summer salad — light and refreshing with a nice balance of flavors covering both sweet and salty. The citrus adds a wonderful tang that will leave you wanting more.

Spicy Orange Vinaigrette:
¾ cup fresh orange juice
3 tablespoons balsamic vinegar
1 tablespoon spicy mustard
1 tablespoon raw agave nectar
1 tiny pinch cayenne pepper
2 pinches sea salt
2 pinches freshly ground black pepper
1½ tablespoons extra-virgin olive oil

Salad:
about 4 slices prosciutto
1 whole cantaloupe, peeled and cut into bite-size pieces
1 whole orange, peeled and sectioned
½ cup sliced almonds or chopped walnuts
¼ cup sliced red onions
about 2 cups spicy baby arugula

Make the dressing first, so it can chill while you prepare the salad. In a blender, place orange juice, balsamic vinegar, mustard, agave nectar, cayenne, salt, and pepper. Hit pulse for about 15–20 seconds. Hit blend while streaming in olive oil. Mix well. Store in an airtight glass jar in the refrigerator. The dressing keeps for up to 2 weeks.

To make the salad, preheat oven to 350°F. Place prosciutto on a slightly oiled baking sheet and bake until crisp, about 10 minutes.

While prosciutto bakes, mix together cantaloupe, orange, nuts, red onion, and arugula in a serving bowl.

When prosciutto is done, let cool, then cut into bite-size strips to top your salad.

To serve, drizzle salad with orange vinaigrette.

Serves 2–4

Growing Together:
Organic Goodness

"Growing foods" — organic nutritious whole foods that give our bodies strength and vitality — are the basis for conscious family cooking. It's important for families to know why to choose organic foods. Why not start by talking with our children about safe, healthy, tasty choices?

Organic foods are grown without the use of pesticides or synthetic chemicals. While we still don't know the full effects that these products can have on our bodies, we do know that the systems of little children are more easily weakened by toxins. We should all be consuming the purest foods possible, but it is especially critical for children's growing bodies.

Organic foods are better for the environment, taste better, and most important, are not saturated in pesticides or chemicals that are potentially very harmful to our health.

Rainbow Eating and Gardening

Eating different colored fresh fruits and veggies is what rainbow eating is all about. It's an easy way to ensure that your body is getting the right amount of nutrients that it needs during various seasons of the year. My family and I take trips to the local farmers' market to buy a variety of colored fruit and vegetable seeds and seedlings at the beginning of each season. We lay them out like a rainbow (you may need to look at the picture on the seed packets to see exactly what color the final fruits and vegetables will be) and decide what we want to grow in our family's rainbow garden.

Roasted Tomato Garden Tacos

During one of the marathon photo shoots for this book, my photographer, Alexandra, my assistant, Amy, and I were working so hard that we suddenly realized we had forgotten to eat lunch. I quickly pulled some tomatoes, cilantro, and scallions from the garden, picked an avocado, and ran to the kitchen to create these easy, scrumptious tacos. It really proved to me how inspiring a home garden can be. Avocados are packed with essential fats, and an average avocado contains about 4 grams of protein. Green tomatoes are their own variety and are highly coveted by chefs. They often have a spicy flavor and are fun to grow. These garden tacos are addictive, so be prepared to crave them frequently.

3 ripe Roma tomatoes, sliced
2 green tomatoes, sliced (not unripe red tomatoes, but a fully ripe green variety)
½ bunch scallions, sliced in long pieces
olive oil for drizzling
2 pinches black pepper
8 (6-inch) corn tortillas
1 cup crumbled feta cheese
1 avocado, peeled, pitted, and chopped
hot sauce, for serving

Preheat oven to 350°F.

Place tomato slices and scallions in a ceramic dish. Drizzle with olive oil and season with pepper. Roast for 15–20 minutes, until softened.

Either over an open flame or in a dry cast-iron skillet, heat corn tortillas until browned.

To assemble tacos, add a portion of the roasted tomatoes, scallions, feta cheese, and avocado to each warm tortilla and fold in half. Serve warm with a little hot sauce.

Serves 4

Ham-n-Cheese Panini with Fresh Grapes

When my mother bought us our first panini grill, I made a million sandwiches until everyone got sick of them and made me stop. I would have kept going though, because I love a good sandwich! From my sandwich development trials came this one that Lotus loves. This version adds a little of "nature's candy" to give it a fresh flavor that kids and adults will love.

Cook's Note: If you don't have a panini press, you can use a grill pan and a heavy lid press to hold down the sandwich and get those beautiful grill marks.

mustard (recipe page 154)
2 slices sourdough bread
several slices ham
several slices Havarti cheese
handful of grapes, sliced in half
salad greens

Preheat panini grill or skillet.

Assemble your sandwich: Spread mustard on bread first, then layer ham and cheese and the top slice of bread. Place on panini grill and let cheese melt. Flip sandwich once or twice.

After the sandwich has been grilled, open it up and add your grapes and salad greens (this keeps the sandwich tasting fresh). Serve immediately.

Serves 2

Growing Together:
Best Meat Choices

Unless you are buying certified organic meats, it's likely the meat you are eating has been injected with growth hormones that speed up an animal's growth, and/or antibiotics (necessary due to the unhygienic living conditions and the illnesses these animals often contract as a result of such conditions). The hormones can have a negative impact on human bodies and especially on growing children.

The best meat choices come from animals that have been fed strictly organic vegetarian diets, have never been injected with antibiotics or growth hormones, and live in a stress-free environment where they are not confined to tight living quarters and unable to roam. Be wary of the word "natural" on meat packaging, as there are no regulations for that word, and therefore no consumer safeguards with it.

Simple Quinoa with Peas and Corn

Lotus loves this dish, which is inspired by a snack her teachers make for her class at school. Quinoa is a wonderful midday meal, as it's filled with protein that really gives the children a boost of energy to do what they do best — play! You can use quinoa in a wide variety of ways — sweet or savory — so no matter what the preferences are in your home, you should be able to find a variation right for everyone.

1 cup quinoa

1 cup vegetable broth

1 cup water

2 teaspoons unsalted butter, softened

1 garlic clove, minced

½ cup fresh peas (use frozen if you cannot find fresh)

½ cup fresh corn kernels, sliced off the cob

pinch black pepper

Put quinoa, vegetable broth, and water in a pot, cover, and bring to a boil. After it comes to a rolling boil, turn down the heat to low, and cook quinoa for about 10 minutes, until liquid has evaporated.

While quinoa is cooking, in a skillet, melt 1 teaspoon of butter and sauté garlic with peas and corn until garlic is lightly browned, about 3–4 minutes.

When quinoa is cooked, stir in sautéed peas and corn mixture. Add the other teaspoon of butter and pepper to taste.

Serve warm with your favorite multigrain crackers.

Serves 4

Growing Together:
School Gardens

My children go to a Waldorf school, where even the youngest children are able to garden in their class plots. They grow a variety of vegetables and herbs and eat them fresh during snack time at school. School gardens are a growing trend, and folks like my friend Conor (who owns MinifarmBox) have started to implement programs to get schools to start gardens. MinifarmBox supports the "50:50 build-a-garden program," where a school community comes up with 50% of the cost of creating a school vegetable garden, and Conor will donate the other half. He brings his garden flatbed boxes to the schools and helps the kids plant them. All kids deserve fresh foods. If your child's school doesn't already have an active garden, perhaps you can try approaching the school with a small garden plot proposal and see if classes can rotate taking care of it. Even a small step can make a big impact!

Udon Noodles with Soybeans and Carrots

Most kids love noodles. These are a simple tasty version that I make a lot and put into my kids' lunches. I have to admit that I make a special trip to our local Japanese store to buy the freshest udon noodles I can, because they always taste so much better than packaged brands. Some supermarkets have them in their refrigerated section. Whenever I make Japanese-inspired foods, I always bring more focus to my preparation, as the Japanese cooking philosophy is inspired by meditation and reverence. It reminds me to slow down and remember to put my loving intentions into the food I prepare.

1 tablespoon tamari sauce

½ tablespoon sesame sauce

1 (12-ounce) package fresh udon noodles

1 cup fresh or frozen shelled soybeans

2 carrots, chopped in small pieces (approximately 1 cup)

4 scallions, chopped in small pieces (approximately ¼ cup)

2 pinches garlic powder

1 pinch cayenne pepper

sea salt and black pepper

sesame seeds, for topping

In a wok or deep frying pan over medium heat, combine and heat tamari sauce, sesame sauce, and udon noodles. Stir for 3–4 minutes.

Add soybeans, carrots, scallions, garlic powder, cayenne pepper, and salt and pepper to taste. Stir for another 4–5 minutes until carrots are soft, but not mushy. Top with sesame seeds and serve warm. (To keep warm for your kids' school lunch, use a stainless steel insulated container. I like the ones I find from Life Without Plastic, in the resource section.)

Serves 4

Super Crunch Apple Cranberry Tuna Wrap

Always choose canned tuna that is water-packed, wild-caught, organic albacore tuna. This ensures that the fishing has been sustainably practiced and there is the lowest mercury content and the highest omega-3 possible. The fruit crunch in this recipe provides a refreshed flavor that brightens up the meal and leaves you feeling satisfied.

2 (7-ounce) cans water-packed albacore tuna

¼ cup homemade tofu mayonnaise (recipe page 156)

½ cup chopped onion

2 stalks celery, finely chopped

¼ cup dried cranberries

½ cup chopped apple, skins on or off

1 hard-boiled egg, chopped

sea salt and black pepper

2 (10-inch) whole grain tortilla wraps

In a large bowl, mix together tuna, mayonnaise, onion, celery, cranberries, apple, and egg. Add salt and pepper to taste. Spoon half the mixture into a tortilla and roll up. Repeat with the second tortilla and the remaining filling. Cut each tortilla in half to serve.

Serve immediately.

Serves 2–4

Cooking Together:
Random Celebrations

Randomly, we will pick a day and call it "Zoë" day, for example. That day will be all about him and, as a family, we will also cook his favorite meal (usually for Zoë it's homemade calzones, corn soup, and freshly baked garlic bread). We do this for all the kids twice a year and never on their birthdays. Our kids look forward to their special days, and not knowing when it will be adds a little suspense and spice to life. You might also consider celebrating special accomplishments, like the first day completed at school, a project completed, or even first steps for a little one, with a special family meal.

Almond Butter and Raspberry Agave Jam (homemade of course!)

Move over PB&J, there is a new classic in town. Almond butter and jam are easy to make and also make great gifts. I suggest serving almond butter and raspberry agave jam on rustic bread or crackers.

Almond Butter:
2 cups raw almonds
1–2 pinches sea salt
1½ teaspoons coconut oil

Raspberry Agave Jam:
3 cups fresh raspberries
1 cup raw agave nectar
juice of ½ lemon

To make the almond butter, preheat oven to 350°F.

On a baking sheet, toast almonds for 8–10 minutes (this brings out their nutty flavor).

In a food processor, blend toasted almonds and salt for about 10–13 minutes. The mixture will first look like a powder, but then the natural oils will be released from the nuts and the texture will become smooth. Add coconut oil to give it a little extra creaminess. Blend to your preferred texture. Almond butter is best stored in an airtight glass jar in the refrigerator. It will last up to 3 months if properly stored.

To make the jam, crush the raspberries first. In a big soup pot on medium heat, heat crushed raspberries for about 2 minutes, then bring to a boil. Add agave nectar and stir mixture for another 2 minutes. Add lemon juice and immediately remove pot from the heat. Continue to stir for another 2 minutes.

Cool, then store in a glass jar. Let jam sit in the refrigerator for 24 hours before using. It will firm up.

Makes 1 (12-ounce) jar of almond butter and 1 (8-ounce) jar of jam

Growing Together: Garden Smoothies

Lotus loves creating what she calls "garden smoothies." She picks various herbs, fruits, and veggies from our garden, combines them with some coconut milk in the blender, hits purée, and sees what she comes up with. This is a fun way to get children inventing snacks straight from the garden. Some of our favorite garden items to include are strawberries, cherry tomatoes, leafy greens, basil, and lemongrass. We freeze leftover smoothies to make delicious popsicles. If you need inspiration, check out my book *Ice Pop Joy* for plenty of ideas on healthy and fun pops to freeze.

Cooking Together:
Zen Lettuce Story

I learned a lot about conscious cooking at the Zen Buddhist community, Tassajara. One of my favorite memories from that period involves me, four HUGE tubs of lettuce, and a quest for the perfect salad. On my first day in the kitchen, I was put at a table outside (overlooking beautiful Carmel Valley), with four enormous bins of lettuce, and was told to separate each piece of lettuce from any wilted pieces and to make sure there were not ANY wilted pieces in the salad that we were going to serve to the guests that evening for dinner. Oh, and I was do this in silence. Boy, I went through all kinds of emotions, from feeling frustrated to annoyed to bored out of my mind, until finally a miraculous thing happened. I fell in love with the lettuce, and it somehow became my personal quest to make sure every piece of lettuce was crisp and beautiful and that the salad that night was filled with my positive loving feelings. This activity took me several hours, and that night when the guests were served those salads, it was one of the proudest moments in my life. The simplicity of taking on a task like separating lettuce leaves shaped the way I create food now. I try very hard to always remember that experience and know that when I pour my heart into my food, whether I am cooking for myself, my family, or a community of folks, the love that went into it can actually be tasted.

Light Lunch Fresh Greens with Lemon-Orange Vinaigrette

When I was a student at Tassajara Zen Center in Carmel Valley, I ate a soup, fresh salad, and some type of delicious homemade bread every day for lunch. It really is the perfect midday meal. There are days when a quick salad is all I have time for, and this one is especially delicious with its perfect balance of flavors and textures.

Lemon-Orange Vinaigrette:
¼ cup fresh lemon juice
¼ cup fresh orange juice
1 garlic clove, minced
1½ teaspoons Dijon mustard
¼ teaspoon sea salt
½ teaspoon black pepper
½ cup olive oil

Salad:
1 bowl fresh greens (from your garden if possible)
½ cup feta cheese
½ cup raw pistachios
½ red onion, chopped
1 cup pomegranate seeds

To make the vinaigrette, in a small bowl whisk together lemon juice, orange juice, garlic, Dijon mustard, salt, and pepper. Slowly pour in the olive oil while whisking at the same time. Vinaigrette can be stored in the refrigerator in a glass container with an airtight lid for up to 2 weeks.

To make the salad, in a large bowl, lightly toss together greens, feta cheese, pistachios, onion, and pomegranate seeds.

To serve, shake vinaigrette, drizzle onto salad, and toss.

Serves 4

Mini Chicken Satay Bites with Spicy Peanut Dressing on a Bed of Red Quinoa

This recipe is great for kids, because the chicken bites are a mini version of satay that can be easily eaten. Add the super grain high-protein red quinoa, and you have a stellar dish. Thai food has a wonderful way of marrying sweet and spicy flavors, and this is a classic that everyone loves.

Chicken Satay:
3 boneless, skinless chicken breasts
bamboo skewers
3 tablespoons coconut oil
1 teaspoon chili powder
1 teaspoon coriander powder
2 teaspoons turmeric powder
4 shallots, chopped
2 garlic cloves, diced
juice of 1 lime
1 teaspoon oyster sauce

Quinoa:
1 cup red quinoa
1 cup vegetable broth
1 cup water

1 garlic clove, whole and peeled
1 tablespoon unsalted butter, softened
1 pinch black pepper

Spicy Peanut Dressing:
½ cup unsalted, unsweetened peanut butter
1 tablespoon coconut milk
2 teaspoons sesame oil
1 teaspoon chili garlic sauce
4 teaspoons rice vinegar
2 tablespoons low-sodium soy sauce
1 teaspoon sesame seeds
1 tablespoon minced fresh cilantro
½ teaspoon garlic powder
juice of 1 lime

To make the satay, cut chicken meat into small cubes, and thread them onto the skewers.

In a food processor, combine coconut oil, chili powder, coriander, turmeric, shallots, garlic, lime juice, and oyster sauce. Pulse until it makes a pastelike mixture. Pour mixture into a container large enough to hold all the skewers. Add the skewers and let them marinate in the refrigerator for 2–4 hours.

Preheat grill while preparing the quinoa and the peanut dressing.

To make the quinoa, put quinoa, vegetable broth, water, garlic clove, butter, and pepper in a pot. Cover and bring to a boil. After it comes to a rolling boil, turn down the heat to low, and cook quinoa for about 10 minutes, until liquid has evaporated. Take out the garlic clove and set quinoa aside until chicken is ready.

To make the dressing, in a food processor, mix all ingredients together and pulse until blended to a smooth consistency. Set aside until chicken is ready.

Grill skewers for about 3–4 minutes on each side. To serve, spoon a bed of red quinoa on each plate, add some chicken pieces on top, and put a bowl of the dipping sauce on the side.

Serves 4

Greening Together: 10 Ways to Green Your Kitchen

Here are some quick tips on how to turn your kitchen "green"!

- Start by claiming your space as your own. Create a sacred space in your kitchen to help remind you to pour all your love into the food you make for your family.

- Start slowly, but begin to replace your plastic containers with glass or stainless steel containers. Keep the BPA out of your home.

- Use organic cleaning products or make your own.

- Start replacing your old cookware with eco-pots and pans. There are many companies that sell "green" cookware.

- Always use your nice plates and cloth napkins and stay away from using plastics. For babies, I use Nova Naturals enamel dishes.

- Use energy-efficient appliances that run on less energy.

- Fill up the sink with water to wash dishes, rather than letting the water constantly run.

- Cook with lids on, rather than off. Cooking with lids off loses three times the amount of energy.

- Compost your food waste! There are small compost buckets you can keep right on your counter for easier use.

- Stop buying plastic water bottles, and instead buy one refillable bottle per person in the household.

Family Favorite Dinners

Dinners are a sacred time in my home. With busy days, it's hard to get good quality time in with each other, and dinner is the perfect meal to sit down, break bread with one another, and talk about our day. We start our meal off by saying a Waldorf verse, then we light a candle and enjoy our meal together. Meals with a baby, preschooler, kindergartner, and teenager can be interesting and it's really fun to hear about the special things that happened in their day. I also believe that no matter what their ages, it's important to have the table looking beautiful with real dishes, cloth napkins, and a fresh flower or herb arrangement. This sets up an environment that brings reverence along with it, and allows the children to see food and the experience of eating together as a comforting, beautiful part of the day's rhythm. This practice also helps little ones get used to the idea of using a mealtime as an opportunity to really connect with others, in meaningful ways.

A Waldorf-Inspired Meal Blessing

Our family meals start with being thankful for what we have. We love this simple Earth blessing, and even Bodhi can say it along with us.

Hands together
Hands apart
Hands together
We're ready to start
Earth who gives to us this food
Sun who makes it ripe and good
Dear Sun, Dear Earth
By you we live
Our loving thanks to you we give!
Blessings on our meal

Anni's Favorite French Onion Soup

Every time it rains, I want this soup. I am not sure why, but it's just so hearty and warm and feels like a complete meal. When I make this soup for dinner, we always have a side vegetable like asparagus and some easy greens with a light vinaigrette. This is the kind of food I love to eat — simple, comforting, and delicious.

1 tablespoon extra-virgin olive oil
2 yellow onions, sliced
3 fresh slices whole grain bread (or your preferred bread)
2 cups water
1 (32-ounce) container beef broth
1 chicken bouillon cube
¼ teaspoon garlic powder
1 bay leaf
1 sprig fresh thyme
2 pinches sea salt
2 pinches black pepper
½ cup freshly shredded Parmesan cheese
8 thin slices Provolone or Havarti cheese

Preheat oven to 350°F.

In a big soup pot or Dutch oven, heat olive oil over medium heat. Add onions and sauté until lightly browned, about 15 minutes.

Meanwhile, cut bread into crouton-sized cubes, spread them in a single layer on a slightly oiled baking sheet, and lightly brown in preheated oven for about 5 minutes. No need to flip over. Take out and set aside.

Add water, broth, bouillon cube, and all spices to the pot, and bring to a boil. Let simmer on medium-low for about 15–20 minutes, until flavors are melded together nicely (keep tasting).

Turn on broiler. Scoop soup, without bay leaf, into 3-inch-deep ceramic bowls or, for little children, 2-inch-deep ramekins, and fill about three-quarters full. Lay toasted bread on top of each dish. Top each with shredded Parmesan cheese and a thin slice

of cheese, letting it hang over the sides of the bowls.

Broil for about 5–8 minutes, until cheese is melted and golden brown. Let bowl cool slightly before handing to a child, but serve warm, while the cheese is nice and gooey.

Serves 8

Tim's Favorite Mushroom and Onion Tart

My husband LOVES mushrooms and onions, and if he could, I think he'd live off pizza. He is from Philly, where everyone seems to just love pizza. This is a light version of a pizza with a puff pastry dough and a beautifully fresh flavor.

Cook's Note: If you have a pizza stone, use it. It helps the crust get a little crispy. If not, you can use a round baking sheet.

olive oil

½ cup chopped shiitake mushrooms (or your favorite variety)

1 yellow onion, in long slices

1 puff pastry sheet, chilled, not frozen

pizza sauce (your favorite)

handful fresh oregano

1 teaspoon dried basil

1 garlic clove, finely minced

red pepper flakes, to taste

½ cup (2 ounces) shredded mozzarella cheese

¼ cup (1 ounce) freshly grated Parmesan cheese

Preheat oven to 350°F.

In a skillet over medium-low heat, heat a small amount of olive oil, then gently sauté mushrooms and onions until browned. Set aside while you prepare the tart crust.

On a floured surface, roll puff pastry into a large circle, about 15 inches across. Using a fork, poke a few times in the center of the dough. Smooth out about an inch-wide border around the edge of the dough.

Spread pizza sauce over surface of dough, leaving that 1-inch edge uncovered. Sprinkle sauce with mushrooms, onions, herbs, garlic, red pepper flakes, and cheeses. Bake for about 15 minutes, until cheese is bubbling and slightly browned. Let cool before slicing.

Serves 2 adults or 4 children

Cooking Together:
Planning a Family Cooking Day

Every week we plan a family cooking day, and each one of our children participates in preparing the meal. A family favorite is making homemade cinnamon rolls in the morning and dough for homemade pizzas for dinner. The kids love putting together their individual favorites. We often end up having a family picnic on a blanket on the living room floor. It's a messy day, but the smiles at the end of the experience make it all worth it!

Grilled Lemon Caper Halibut

Halibut is a light and flaky saltwater fish with a wonderful subtle flavor. This recipe is tasty and comforting and goes nicely with a simple green salad with a vinaigrette dressing. If halibut is not readily available, try another white flaky fish such as tilapia.

1 tablespoon extra-virgin olive oil, plus more for oiling pan

2 Alaskan halibut fillets (approximately 8 ounces each)

juice of 2 lemons

1 garlic clove, minced

sea salt and black pepper

1 pinch cayenne pepper

1 tablespoon capers

1 tablespoon unsalted butter

Wipe a grill pan thoroughly with oil. (Halibut is somewhat delicate, so your grill pan must be well oiled so the fish won't stick and then fall apart.) Heat pan over medium heat.

Season fillets on both sides with lemon juice (reserving some for finished fish), 1 tablespoon olive oil, garlic, salt and pepper to taste, and cayenne.

Add approximately half the capers and half the butter to the grill pan, place fillets on top of them, and begin to grill. Flip the fish after about 4 minutes and add remaining capers and butter. The fish should be fully cooked after about 10 minutes.

Before serving, add more lemon juice to fish if desired.

Serves 4

Linguine with Spicy Tomato Caper Sauce

Most kids love pasta, and my children are no exception. I like to find new and creative ways to prepare it, such as with this fresh tomato sauce. Even my pickiest eater, Bodhi, loves this pasta dish. Try serving it with rustic Parmesan cheese bread (use the recipe on page 94).

1 tablespoon olive oil for boiling noodles, plus 1 tablespoon for sauce
sea salt
13 ounces (¾ package) linguine pasta
2 garlic cloves, minced
2 cups halved grape tomatoes
¼ cup capers
juice of 1 small lemon
¼ teaspoon red pepper flakes (less if you want it less spicy)
1 cup freshly grated Parmesan cheese, divided
black pepper

In a large soup pot, bring 6 cups water, 1 tablespoon olive oil, and 2 pinches of sea salt to a boil. Add linguine and boil for 7–8 minutes until al dente.

While water is coming to a boil, make the tomato caper sauce. In a large skillet, on medium heat, cover bottom of pan with olive oil, about 1 tablespoon. Add garlic and sauté for about 2 minutes. Add tomatoes, capers, lemon juice, red pepper flakes, ½ cup Parmesan cheese, and salt and pepper. Stir together and sauté for about 5–7 minutes, until flavors have melded together. Add more olive oil if desired.

Pour sauce over cooked and drained linguine and top with the rest of the cheese.

Serves 4

Vine-Roasted Tomato Soup with Warmed Tortillas

Tomatoes are one of my favorite foods. This soup is very easy to pull together, which makes it a great meal for the kids to help me make. Every Wednesday Bodhi makes soup in his class, and all the little ones help cut the vegetables and prepare the soup. This is a practice that not only feeds their tummies, but helps them develop some skills in the kitchen.

4 fresh vine-ripened tomatoes
sea salt and black pepper
1 tablespoon unsalted butter
1 medium yellow onion, diced
2 garlic cloves, finely diced
1 (32-ounce) container vegetable broth
1 (15-ounce) can diced tomatoes
1 (15-ounce) can crushed tomatoes
¼ cup fresh corn kernels, for topping
handful of toasted pumpkin seeds, for topping (recipe page 53)
2 sprigs fresh cilantro, for topping
corn tortillas, heated and browned

Preheat oven to 375°F.

Cut tomatoes in half and lightly season with salt and pepper. Place in a ceramic dish and roast for about 15 minutes, until nice and soft.

In a skillet over medium heat, melt butter, then sauté onion and garlic until caramelized, about 4–5 minutes.

In a large soup pot, combine vegetable broth, diced and crushed tomatoes, whole roasted tomatoes (skins and all), salt and pepper to taste, and sautéed onions and garlic. Bring to a boil, then reduce heat to low and simmer for about 20 minutes.

While the soup is simmering, cook corn kernels in a skillet until browned, about 5 minutes. Set aside for use as a topping.

Pour soup into blender, and hit pulse only once to leave it a little chunky. (This also works with an immersion blender.)

Pour into bowls, and top with roasted corn kernels, pumpkin seeds, and cilantro. Serve immediately, with warmed tortillas.

Serves 5

Growing Together:
Veggie Stands

Growing fresh foods is great for our health and can be more affordable than buying your fresh organic foods from the grocery. During one growing season, a small 4 x 4-foot garden can produce up to 70 heads of lettuce, 80 pounds of tomatoes, dozens of eggplants, zucchini, melons, beets, and beans, and the list goes on and on!

My kids are always impressed by how much we can grow ourselves. They often hold "Veggie Stands" (think lemonade stand with garden vegetables instead of small cups of lemonade) to sell a little produce to our friends and neighbors.

Veggie Sliders with Blue Corn Chips

Having one vegetarian in the house means that we always have to make sure that we have a meat alternative for dinner. Zoë has been a vegetarian his entire life, and we like to honor the different food preferences in our home by providing something for everyone. This recipe is so tasty that even if you love meat, you won't miss it in these!

8 blue corn tortillas

2 tablespoons olive oil, divided

sea salt

¼ cup black beans (canned or fully cooked)

¼ cup diced yellow onion

¼ cup diced fresh green bell pepper

¼ cup diced fresh zucchini

1 carrot, diced

3 tablespoons whole wheat bread crumbs

1 tablespoon whole wheat flour

1½ garlic cloves, minced

1 teaspoon hemp seed powder (use your coffee grinder)

1 teaspoon sesame seed powder (use your coffee grinder)

pinch cayenne pepper

black pepper

Gouda cheese slices, to melt on burger

handful of fresh sprouts; 1 fresh tomato, sliced in rings; 1 red onion, sliced in rings

Thousand Island dressing (your favorite brand)

To make the tortilla chips, preheat oven to 350°F. Brush top side of blue corn tortillas with 1 table-spoon olive oil, and cut into triangular pieces. Place on baking sheets and bake for 8–10 minutes, until crisp. Sprinkle with a little sea salt and set aside until ready to use. (They should stay crisp while preparing the rest of the meal.)

To make the veggie sliders, mash black beans to a chunky consistency. In a large bowl, combine beans, all veggies, bread crumbs, flour, garlic, hemp seed powder, sesame seed powder, cayenne, and salt and pepper to taste. Knead ingredients together with your hands until you can form a ball. Form into small patties.

In a skillet, heat 1 tablespoon oil over medium heat. Cook veggie patties for 4–5 minutes on each side. Once you flip burgers to second side, cover with cheese slice to melt.

Dress burgers with all condiments and serve with warm blue corn tortilla chips.

Serves 8

Broccoli and Cheese Soup with Pistachio-Crusted Parmesan Cheese Bread

On a cold day, nothing is better than soup. It's warm and comforting and just makes you feel good. This is a classic combination that kids love and is easy to whip up for dinner. Leftovers are perfect for the next day's school lunch. If you are sending hot foods to school with your children, try the Sanctus Mundo stainless steel wide-mouthed containers. They work great! You can buy them online. We use them every day.

Soup:
2 tablespoons (¼ stick) unsalted butter
1 yellow onion, chopped
2 garlic cloves, minced
1 teaspoon fresh thyme
4 yellow potatoes, peeled and cubed
1 head fresh broccoli, chopped
2 cups milk
1 cup heavy cream
sea salt and black pepper

1 cup (4 ounces) shredded cheddar cheese
½ cup chopped walnuts, for topping
sour cream, for topping

Bread:
rustic bread, any kind you like, thickly sliced
2 garlic cloves, sliced in half
½ cup freshly grated Parmesan cheese
½ cup finely chopped pistachios
unsalted butter, for serving (optional)

Growing Together:
Healthy Dairy — 3 Moos for No BGH!

Conventionally grown dairy products come from cows that are regularly fed BGH (Bovine Growth Hormone) to increase their daily milk supply. This is often painful for the cows and can cause udder infections, which can also spread to the milk. These cows are also given antibiotics regularly to increase growth, which are used in an effort to compensate for unsanitary living environments.

Organically grown dairy comes from cows that are NEVER fed BGH or antibiotics. They are free to roam in the fresh air and graze naturally on vegetarian feed. Not only is this more humane, it's better for the environment and human bodies, especially growing children.

You may even want to be adventurous and try raw milk. This is milk that is straight from the cow or goat, has not been pasteurized, and maintains all the healthy enzymes. Is it safe? You bet, as long as you get the milk from a farmer whose cows are grass-fed and live in sanitary living conditions. Talk with your local raw milk provider about her farming practices. You won't believe the taste difference. It is very creamy and super delicious.

To make the soup, in a soup pot, melt butter over medium heat. Add onion and sauté until tender, about 5 minutes. Add garlic, thyme, potatoes, and broccoli, and sauté for another 5 minutes. Add milk and heavy cream, and bring to a gentle boil. Add salt and pepper to taste. Reduce heat and simmer the soup for 15 minutes, until potatoes are soft. Add cheese and continue to simmer for 2 minutes.

While soup is cooking, make the Pistachio-Crusted Bread. Rub cut sides of halved garlic cloves over each piece of bread. Top each piece with a handful of Parmesan cheese and pistachios. Toast until browned, either in toaster oven or under a broiler. If desired, serve bread with butter.

Purée soup mixture in a blender or food processor. Serve hot with a sprinkling of walnuts and a small dollop of sour cream on top of each serving. Serve with Pistachio-Crusted Bread.

Serves 6

Grilled Shrimp and Brown Rice

Grilled shrimp is one of my favorite dishes, and Lotus loves it, too. This recipe is an easy-to-make and tasty dinner if you are running late and want to make a quick meal. I often add ground chia seeds to my rice, as they give a huge boost of fiber, protein, and calcium. They also contain more iron than spinach does!

Rice:

4 cups water

1 cup brown rice, well rinsed

1 pat unsalted butter

1 whole garlic clove

pinch sea salt and black pepper

1 tablespoon chia seed powder (use your coffee grinder; optional)

Shrimp:

1 pound fresh raw jumbo or tiger shrimp, peeled and cleaned

juice of 1 lemon, plus extra wedges for serving

1 tablespoon olive oil

2 garlic cloves, minced

pinch sea salt and black pepper

¼ cup chopped fresh cilantro

To make the rice, in a saucepan over high heat, bring water to a boil. Add brown rice, butter, whole garlic clove, and a little salt and pepper. Turn heat down to medium and simmer, uncovered, for about 30–35 minutes.

Drain rice and put back on stove (no flame and in the same pot), covered, for 10–12 minutes to let settle. Add chia seed powder, if using, and mix.

To cook the shrimp, oil your grill pan thoroughly and heat it on medium-high heat. In a large bowl, season shrimp with lemon juice, olive oil, minced garlic, salt, pepper, and cilantro. Grill shrimp for about 2 minutes on each side, until pink.

Serve shrimp with brown rice and lemon wedges.

Serves 4

Cooking Together:
Conscious Community Cooking

I learned how to cook at a Zen Buddhist community called Tassajara, in Carmel Valley, California. They taught me the art of conscious community cooking, where each of us was responsible for one ingredient, and we had to put our full love and attention to it, whether it was chopping tomatoes, picking over lettuce leaves, baking, or cooking rice. That's because it's all sacred, every job. Bringing our presence and full awareness to our cooking and allowing our children to have special jobs in the kitchen ends up creating a community meal that is filled with love and tastes great. I have found that this lesson also translates to other aspects of our lives. The more we practice living in the moment, the more we appreciate each one.

Growing Together:
Baby Food Garden

My friend Conor is an expert gardener. He started a cool business called MinifarmBox. He travels to people's homes and builds plant boxes for them while teaching them about gardening. I was working on a garden box with Conor one day (I happened to be pregnant at the time), when he had an idea to make baby food gardens. Together we created the perfect garden for making baby food. With a little preplanning, your baby's first veggies can be ready to harvest when he or she is ready to start eating solid foods. Imagine the first foods you feed your baby to be ones that you grew specifically for him or her! Our plant suggestions include sweet potatoes, butternut and other winter squash, carrots, kale, English peas, potatoes, and various herbs. Planting a first foods garden in your baby's honor is a wonderful way to make sure you know exactly what your baby is eating and to keep it as fresh and organic as possible.

Nurturing Butternut Squash Soup with Parmesan Crisps

Butternut squash has a sweet, nutty flavor and is an amazing food, rich in vitamins A and C and easy to grow in a home vegetable patch. Kids like growing this hearty vegetable because it can grow to a large size, which feels like a real accomplishment. When roasted and puréed, butternut squash is a great first food for babies and can be turned into many wonderful dishes for the entire family.

Soup:

1 tablespoon extra-virgin olive oil

1 butternut squash (approximately 3 pounds), peeled and cubed

1 yellow onion, chopped

3 garlic cloves, chopped

1 carrot, peeled and chopped

1 (32-ounce) container chicken broth

½ cup milk

1 cup water

¼ teaspoon freshly grated nutmeg

2 leaves fresh sage, left whole

sea salt and freshly ground black pepper

1 pat butter

1 cup (4 ounces) stemmed and chopped shiitake mushrooms, for topping

2 tablespoons ricotta, for topping

Crisps:

2 cups (8 ounces) freshly grated Parmesan cheese

To make the soup, in a soup pot over medium heat, heat oil. Add butternut squash, onion, garlic, and carrot, and sauté for about 8 minutes. Add chicken broth, milk, and water. Season with nutmeg, sage, and salt and pepper to taste. Bring to a boil.

Reduce heat and simmer soup for 15–20 minutes or until vegetables are thoroughly cooked through and soft.

While soup is simmering, make Parmesan crisps. Preheat oven to 350°F.

Take 2 tablespoons of Parmesan cheese and pat down firmly on a parchment-lined baking sheet. Make as many as you can using the full amount of cheese. Bake for about 6–8 minutes, until golden brown. Let crisps cool and harden while finishing the soup.

Remove sage leaves and pour soup mixture into blender and blend to desired texture. Cover and set aside.

Heat skillet over medium heat, melt a pat of butter, and sauté mushrooms until soft, about 4–5 minutes. Add a pinch of salt and a pinch of pepper.

Serve soup warm, topped with warm mushrooms and a dollop of ricotta, and with a Parmesan crisp on the side.

Serves 4–6

BBQ Chicken

This chicken is fun to make when you are having guests for a summer dinner. If serving a big crowd, double the recipe. For a full feast, serve this chicken with a garden salad, corn on the cob with herbed butter (recipe page 150), rustic bread, and berry tarts (recipe page 142) for dessert.

Cook's Note: You can prepare the BBQ sauce in advance and refrigerate it overnight.

BBQ Sauce:
½ cup homemade catsup (recipe page 155)
3 garlic cloves, minced
½ cup light brown sugar
juice of ½ lemon
juice of ½ grapefruit
½ tablespoon chia seed powder (use your coffee grinder)
½ tablespoon wheat germ
1 teaspoon hot sauce
3 tablespoons Dijon mustard
¼ cup blackstrap molasses
¼ cup cider vinegar
sea salt and black pepper
8 chicken drumsticks

To prepare the BBQ sauce, in a saucepan combine catsup, garlic, brown sugar, lemon juice, grapefruit juice, chia seed powder, wheat germ, hot sauce, mustard, molasses, vinegar, and salt and pepper to taste. Bring to a boil. Reduce heat to medium-low and let simmer for about 10 minutes, until flavors meld. Mix well. Set aside to use when needed.

Preheat grill pan or barbecue grill.

In a shallow dish, coat chicken with BBQ sauce and let sit for about 10–15 minutes. Grill chicken for 10–15 minutes, turning frequently. Brush with sauce as you flip and grill the chicken. Test for doneness and grill an additional 5 minutes if needed.

Serves 4

Greening Together:
Make Your Own Cleaner

Here's a simple recipe for an all-purpose cleaner that can help you save money and keep the toxins found in most commercial cleaning products out of your home.

Mix ½ cup vinegar, ¼ cup baking soda, ½ gallon (2 liters) water, the juice of 1 whole lemon, and 1 teaspoon lavender essential oil. Once combined, store in plastic BPA-free bottle.

Kindergarten Stone Soup

Lotus's kindergarten class made "stone soup" for the parents on Thanksgiving. The children take part in choosing the stones, preparing the soup, baking the bread, decorating, and serving. The basic outline of the story of Stone Soup is that one person can bring a whole community together by starting to create a soup with nothing but water and stones. Others gather and each adds a single simple ingredient to the mix. As a community gathers, the soup becomes more savory, and then all share this incredible soup together. Why not host a stone soup party in your neighborhood or with a group of friends?

1 tablespoon unsalted butter

1 yellow onion, chopped

3 garlic cloves, chopped

2 (32-ounce) containers vegetable broth

2 chicken bouillon cubes

3 cups water

3 medium-sized stones, scrubbed clean

2 fresh zucchini, chopped

3 fresh tomatoes, chopped

3 fresh carrots, chopped

3 stalks celery, chopped

1½ cups chopped fresh green beans (optional)

sea salt and black pepper

1 (8-ounce) package small pasta shells

In a large soup pot over medium-low heat, melt butter. Add onion and garlic, and sauté for about 6 minutes.

Raise the heat and add vegetable broth, bouillon cubes, water, stones, zucchini, tomatoes, carrots, celery, and green beans. Season with salt and pepper to taste. Bring soup to a boil, then turn heat to low and simmer for 30 minutes. Add the pasta shells to the soup after the vegetables have simmered for about 20 minutes. Soup is ready when vegetables are well cooked through and soft.

Ladle soup into bowls and serve immediately.

Serves 15–20

Cooking Together: Show & Tell

When Zoë was in the primary grades, we dedicated one day a month to going into the classroom and talking with the kids about various food topics including organic cooking, growing foods, and eating fresh and locally. We would also invite the children to make a recipe, and we would bring ingredients with us to show them some simple cooking ideas. This tradition not only expanded the culinary palates of the children, but it connected us more to the school community. The kids loved learning how to make fresh guacamole! If you can, volunteer in your child's classroom and show off some of your homegrown fruits or vegetables and fun ways to prepare them.

Whole Roasted Herb Chicken with Roasted Veggies and Dark Chocolate Dipping Sauce

This meal was inspired by my all-time favorite movie, Chocolat. I love the scene where everything they are eating at dinner is dipped in warm chocolate sauce. Since I have two real chocolate lovers in the house, this chicken dish seems like a perfectly decadent meal to serve on special occasions. The tradition in our home is that if you are invited for our chocolate chicken dinner, you add a blessing of gratitude to our "Gratitude Jar" and read it at dinner. We figure that if we are able to indulge in warm dark chocolate sauce, fresh garden vegetables, and chicken, we are blessed and should acknowledge it.

1 (6–8 pound) whole chicken
1 tablespoon unsalted butter for outside, plus 2 tablespoons for inside cavity
sea salt and black pepper
juice of 2 lemons
4 whole garlic cloves
3 sprigs fresh rosemary
1 sprig fresh thyme
10 small carrots, left whole (if larger carrots, use 5 and cut in half)
10 yellow baby potatoes, halved
1 yellow onion, sliced
4 fresh Roma tomatoes, halved
1 tablespoon olive oil
4 ounces dark chocolate, melted
pinch cayenne pepper

Preheat oven to 450°F. Wash chicken and clean out cavity. Rub chicken with 1 tablespoon butter, sea salt, and pepper. Squeeze lemon juice all over chicken. In the cavity, place 2 tablespoons butter, garlic cloves, rosemary, and thyme. Tie legs together with a piece of hemp or kitchen string. Place chicken in a large roasting pan on a rack, which will help cook the chicken more evenly.

Add carrots, potatoes, onions, and tomatoes to the pan, surrounding the chicken. Drizzle them with olive oil and sprinkle with salt and pepper. Cover chicken and veggies with cheesecloth.

Cook for about 35 minutes at 450°F, then decrease oven temperature to 375°F and cook for another 20 minutes. Test for doneness; juice should be clear, not rosy (cut behind the leg to check).

When the chicken is almost finished, melt dark chocolate in the top of a double boiler. Add cayenne to the melting chocolate and stir until chocolate is completely melted and smooth.

Serve chicken and roasted veggies with warm chocolate sauce on the side for dipping.

Serves 4

Growing Together:
Support Local Farming & Sustainability

When you support your local farmer, you cut out the middlemen of distributors and marketers, and you give the farmer more on the dollar for the food he grows. Many of these local farmers are trying to produce organic crops, which are better for our bodies and the environment. When you buy directly from local farmers, the food is fresher, has not been transported long distances, and therefore contains more of the product's original nutritional value. Find opportunities to talk with farmers. Your kids will learn a lot about where their food comes from, how it's grown, and may even get the chance to help harvest something. When you support this sustainable practice, you are looking out for the betterment of our collective future.

Savory Sides

When Tim and I first met, I was a strict vegetarian and ate roasted tomatoes with just about everything. I was shocked that he had never eaten one. In fact, he said most of the vegetables he ate growing up were from a can, and he wasn't sure he liked any fresh veggies. This was literally unbelievable to me, but after some time together, he began to eat fresh foods and started to connect the relationship of food to his feelings.

Our food choices are directly related to our mood, emotions, and spiritual energy. Tim has now learned how these factors are interrelated and actually can affect our happiness. He writes an amazing blog called "Practicing Happy," and in it he talks about these relationships and why they are so important to our overall life satisfaction. Choosing food companions is just as important as choosing whom you will break bread with, and each is a sacred act worth thoughtful contemplation. This chapter features some simple sides that are great with most meals.

Spicy Yellow Potato and Sweet Potato Fries

Kids love fries! This version is baked and lightly spiced and a healthier option than many traditional fried potato recipes. This delicious combo is a great snack or party food and super easy to make. For a rustic-looking table, try using repurposed tin cans for serving the fries. You may also want to use my organic BBQ sauce from the chicken recipe (see page 100), for dipping.

1 teaspoon ground black pepper

¼ teaspoon garlic powder

2 pinches cayenne pepper

pinch sea salt

extra-virgin olive oil

2 yellow potatoes (such as Yukon Golds), peeled and sliced into sticks

2 sweet potatoes, peeled and sliced into sticks

BBQ sauce, warmed, for dipping

Preheat oven to 350°F.

Combine pepper, garlic powder, cayenne pepper, and salt in a bowl with enough extra-virgin olive oil to coat the fries. Place all the potato pieces in the bowl and mix with your hands until they are well coated.

Place potatoes in a single layer over 2 baking sheets, and cook for 15–20 minutes. Flip over once until crisp and ready to serve. Serve with BBQ sauce.

Serves 4 as a snack, serves more as part of a meal

Greening Together: Repurposing

Repurposing old items can be fun, creative, and cost-effective. We save old clothes and turn them into tons of stuff. Knitted socks, old dresses, and well-worn sweaters become play food, balls, purses, pouch necklaces, and cuddly dolls. Empty cans become decorative canisters to hold flowers, paintbrushes, and other art supplies. Egg cartons become paint containers or homes for tiny nature creatures or even faeries.

Growing Together:

Support Community Farmers' Markets

Farmers' markets are an amazing way to connect with your local farmers, talk with folks about what they are growing and how, and buy the freshest produce possible. To encourage my kids to come to the market with me, I give each of them a basket when we go and allow them to buy their morning snacks and keep them in their own baskets. We always end up having snacked our way through the market and leave with fruits, veggies, eggs, cheese, flowers, and happy, full tummies.

Asparagus with Tamari and Almond Slices

Asparagus has been considered a delicacy for centuries. Health-wise, asparagus is high in potassium and folate. The whole stalk can be eaten, and if you are pregnant, eat a lot because the folate will help with the cellular development of your growing baby.

15–20 fresh asparagus stalks
2 tablespoons (¼ stick) unsalted butter
2 tablespoons tamari or low-sodium soy sauce
¼ cup almonds, chopped or sliced
sea salt and black pepper

In a steamer basket, steam asparagus for only 3–5 minutes, keeping it crisp. Dress with butter, tamari (or soy sauce), almond slices, and salt and pepper to taste.

Serves 4

Zoë's Favorite Baked Parmesan-Crusted Artichokes

Zoë and I love artichokes in every form, on pizzas, in dips, in salads, or baked with garlic and Parmesan. Living in California, we can easily get big beautiful artichokes.

2 whole artichokes
4 garlic cloves, minced (2 for each artichoke)
½ cup balsamic vinegar
2 tablespoons (¼ stick) unsalted butter
½ cup freshly grated Parmesan cheese

Preheat oven to 400°F.

Prep artichokes by cutting off stems and slicing about an inch off the top of each one. Then cut down the middle to make two halves. Place, cut side up, on a baking sheet or in an ovenproof dish.

Top each artichoke half equally with garlic, balsamic vinegar, butter, and Parmesan cheese. Bake for 20–25 minutes, until leaves are easy to pull off.

Serve with melted butter or homemade tofu mayonnaise (recipe page 156) to dip leaves into.

Serves 4

Luscious Garlic Beet Chips

I pair these chips with my pastrami bleu cheese sandwich (recipe page 65), and they are delicious. You can also use this recipe for slices of butternut or other winter squash, potatoes, or parsnips.

2 large fresh beets, sliced in chip sizes (use a mandoline for slicing, if you have one)
olive oil
2 whole garlic cloves, halved
pinch cayenne pepper
2 pinches garlic powder
2 pinches sea salt

Preheat oven to 375°F.

Place beet slices in a large bowl and lightly drizzle with olive oil. Add garlic cloves, cayenne pepper, garlic powder, and sea salt. Toss to coat beet slices thoroughly. Arrange beets in a single layer on a baking sheet. Bake for approximately 20 minutes (turning once), until crisp.

Serves 4

Greening Together:
Veggie-Dyed Eggs

In the spring, instead of using store-bought dyes to color your eggs, keep it natural and from the garden. Use your veggies to make natural dyes. My kids LOVE our veggie-dyeing egg day. Boil each kind of vegetable in 4 cups of water, letting the natural colors release from them. Add ½ cup of vinegar to each color before dyeing eggs. Note that these veggies will no longer be edible after boiling down.

We use:

- **Beet roots: red**
- **Black tea: tan**
- **Blueberries: blue**
- **Cinnamon: brown**

- **Coffee: light brown**
- **Kale: green**
- **Onion skins: light yellow**
- **Paprika & Carrots: orange**

- **Raspberries & Strawberries: pink**
- **Turmeric: golden yellow**

Anni's Favorite Roasted Tomatoes

Roasted tomatoes go well with everything, in my opinion. These make a great match with a bowl of brown rice and a piece of cheesy bread with a roasted garlic spread.

small ripe tomatoes, cut in half
olive oil for drizzling on top
a few pinches dried basil
sea salt and crushed black pepper

Preheat oven to 250°F. Line baking sheet with parchment paper.

On the baking sheet, arrange tomatoes a couple of inches apart, cut side up so the juices collect and caramelize in their cups. Drizzle with olive oil and sprinkle with dried basil. Season with sea salt and pepper. Bake for 60 minutes, until lightly browned. Serve warm with your favorite meal.

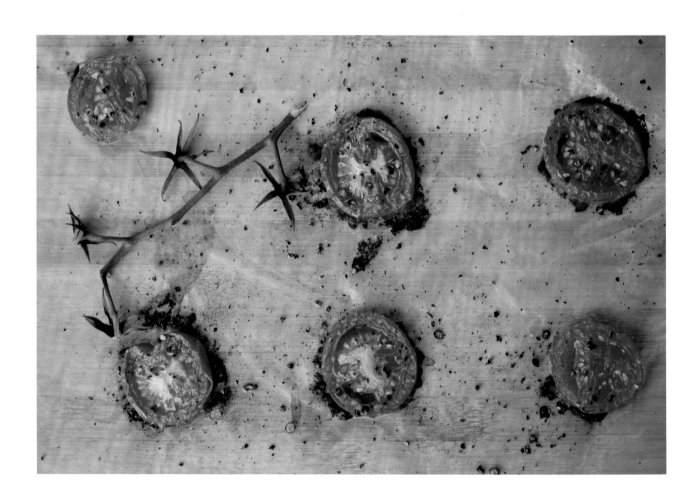

Perfect Roasted Garlic

I first ate roasted garlic at our annual local Renaissance Faire. Once the garlic is fully roasted, you can squeeze the creamy cloves from their papery skins and spread them on bread or crackers for a simple but delicious accompaniment to a meal. I also like to use roasted garlic on pizza or to complement baked cheesy potatoes. It's even great mixed with pasta and a little Parmesan cheese.

Cook's Note: A muffin pan works well for this.

3 full heads garlic
olive oil
freshly ground pepper

Preheat oven to 400°F.

Remove the outermost papery layer from the heads of garlic and cut the tops off the garlic heads. Place garlic heads in muffin cups. Drizzle each one with olive oil, and sprinkle each one with a little ground pepper. Cover each one with foil. Bake for approximately 30 minutes, until nice and soft.

Spread on your favorite bread.

Serves 4

Growing Together:
Kids Composting

Organic matter can be broken down by decay in your compost pile. My kids made this compost project, and it really works! I let Zoë help the little ones roll the compost bin around, kind of like a game.

Make your own compost bin for around $15.00!

Materials:

1. Large plastic trash can with lid that locks on

2. Platform of some sort (I used a wooden plant stand on wheels)

3. Screws (to attach platform to trash can)

4. Drill with large drill bit

What to do:

1. Drill holes in your trash can on each side up and down, on the lid, and on the bottom.

2. In order to elevate the can off the ground, so it can effectively drain, attach a wooden platform.

3. Add organic matter, such as eggshells, fruit and veggie skins, grass trimmings, leaves, and nut shells. Every few days, roll the bin around in the yard to mix it up.

4. In a couple of months or so, you will have nutrient-rich organic matter you can add to your soil to grow your foods!

Compliments of Many Little Blessing Blog

Fig Jam with Garlic Cheese Tarts

These mini tarts look fancy, but are easy to make and seriously delicious. They are the perfect bite before any meal. I buy a great-tasting garlic cheese at my farmers' market. Look in your area for a local or regional version of garlic cheese or another spiced cheese.

unsalted butter
1 sheet puff pastry, chilled, not frozen
unbleached all-purpose flour
½ cup crumbled garlic cheese or another spiced cheese
¼ cup fig jam (recipe page 151)
¼ cup finely chopped walnuts

Preheat oven to 350°F. Grease a mini muffin pan with unsalted butter.

Roll out puff pastry on floured surface, about ¼ inch thick. With a small round cutter, cut 3-inch circles in the dough. (You should get about 20 circles from 1 sheet of pastry.) Press the rounds into the buttered mini muffin cups.

Into each muffin cup, put some crumbled garlic cheese, a dollop of fig jam, and a sprinkling of walnuts. Bake for 10–12 minutes, until lightly browned. Serve nice and warm!

Serves 6

Stuffed Focaccia French Bread

I love making this bread and giving it as gifts to our friends and teachers at the holidays. Making bread creates family traditions that last a lifetime.

Cook's Note: When I make bread, I put a baking pan full of ice in the bottom of the hot oven as I am putting in the bread. This step and the egg wash will give the bread that golden crispy crust you are looking for.

3–4 fresh Roma tomatoes, chopped
3 garlic gloves, minced
1 cup finely chopped fresh basil
1 cup shredded mozzarella cheese
2 tablespoons balsamic vinegar
¼ teaspoon rice wine vinegar
sea salt and ground black pepper
2 tablespoons active dry yeast
2 cups warm water
3 cups all-purpose unbleached flour
2 teaspoons sea salt
2 cups whole wheat pastry flour
olive oil, for wiping bowl
1 egg
1 tablespoon water

Cooking Together:
Herbs & Spices Game

A fun game to play at the supermarket with young children is to give them little note cards with pictures of various herbs and have them locate the herbs in the store. This is a fun way to keep your kids interested in the shopping process, to help them learn about various herbs (you can make the cards with fruits or veggies, too), and to distract them from asking for too many "extras" (moms, you know what I mean!).

Prepare the filling by mixing the tomatoes, garlic, basil, mozzarella, balsamic vinegar, rice wine vinegar, and salt and pepper to taste in a large bowl. Set aside.

In a small bowl, dissolve yeast in warm water until foamy, about 10 minutes.

In the bowl of your electric mixer, place 3 cups all-purpose flour, yeast mixture, and salt. Use your dough hook to mix into a ball. (If you do not have a mixer, use a spoon to mix until it starts to turn into a sticky dough ball, and then use your hands to finish the mixing.) Add whole wheat pastry flour. Mix again into a dough ball.

Remove dough from the mixer bowl and, on a floured surface, knead the dough for about 10 minutes, until it has an elastic texture.

Lightly coat a large bowl with olive oil and put the dough in the bowl, cover with a damp towel, and set aside to rise in a warm area. Let the dough double in size, about 1 hour.

Preheat oven to 400°F. Lightly coat a baking sheet with olive oil spray.

Remove dough from bowl, punch down, and knead again for 5 minutes. Cut dough in half and roll out each half (this type of bread cooks up better in smaller loaves). Spoon tomato filling onto the center of the dough and then roll each side over the filling, until the seams come together. Pinch all seams together with water and carefully flip over the bread onto the prepared pan. (Make sure all seams are well sealed, as you do not want the filling to leak out while cooking. If it does leak out a little, don't freak out, it's still a great bread!)

Make 3 small shallow slices across the top of each roll. Do not cut through the bread. Make an egg wash by combining egg and water in a small bowl. Brush some on the tops of the loaves, then lightly spray with water from a water bottle. Bake for 30–35 minutes, until bread is golden brown. Remove from oven and let cool slightly before slicing. Serve warm with butter.

Makes 2 loaves

All My Love Whole Grain Honey Bread

Whole grain bread is one of the most nourishing things to eat and the perfect complement to soups, salads, and pasta dishes. It's just good all by itself with some delicious honey butter (recipe page 150). At Tassajara, we would make bread every day for lunch and eat it with soup and salad. It's amazing how fulfilling a simple meal like that can be. Always break bread with those you love!

Cook's Note: Have a water bottle and egg wash handy to get a crispy crust on the outside and soft smooth fluffy texture on the inside of your bread.

2 packages active dry yeast

2 cups warm water

¼ cup honey

1 tablespoon flax seed

1 tablespoon wheat germ

2 tablespoons sunflower seeds, ground to a powder (use your coffee grinder)

1 teaspoon sea salt

2 cups whole wheat pastry flour

4 cups unbleached all-purpose flour

olive oil, for wiping bowl

1 egg

1 tablespoon water

In a large mixer bowl, dissolve yeast in warm water until foamy, about 10 minutes.

Add honey, flax seed, wheat germ, sunflower seed powder, and salt. Add whole wheat flour. Mix until it starts forming a ball.

Slowly start to add all-purpose flour, mixing with your dough hook (or your hands) until it forms a ball. Remove dough from bowl and knead with your hands on a floured surface for about 5–7 minutes.

Wipe a large bowl with olive oil. Add dough, cover with a damp towel, and set aside in a warm area. Let the dough double in size, about 35 minutes.

Preheat oven to 375°F.

Remove dough from bowl, punch down, and knead again for 5 minutes. Cut ball in half and shape into 2 equal loaves. Put each loaf into a greased loaf pan. Make 3 shallow slices across top of each loaf. Do not cut through the bread. Make an egg wash by combining egg and water in a small bowl. Brush it over the tops of the loaves, then lightly spray with water from a water bottle.

Bake for 30–35 minutes, until bread is golden brown. Remove bread from oven and then from pans to cool on a wire rack for about 10 minutes. Serve warm with butter, roasted garlic (recipe page 115), or honey butter (recipe page 150).

Makes 2 loaves

Cooking Together:
Fresh Bread Project

One day my husband and I decided that for one year we would make all of our own bread. This seemed daunting at first, but then we came to really enjoy our Sunday evening bread-making, and the kids loved it, too. There is just something about playing with dough that makes kids happy. Since we started this project, we have made all kinds of breads, and this new family tradition has taught our kids that there is something really sacred about sharing bread with loved ones. Try baking your own bread, from scratch — no bread machines — and see how this simple task can bring an extra loaf of love into your home. We have also had bread parties for kids, where they make their own bread in their own terracotta pot! Fresh bread also makes great gifts!

Refreshing Desserts

I don't know many people who don't appreciate a sweet treat now and again. I don't typically use refined sugar in my desserts, but I sometimes sweeten with alternative sugars. Feel free to experiment with these recipes and use whatever you prefer to sweeten your desserts.

My son Bodhi and my husband both have an intense sweet tooth. If left unattended, these two could definitely eat more treats than they should. Zoë likes sour and bitter-tasting desserts; Bodhi and Tim prefer chocolate anything; and Lotus, who is not particularly discriminating, tends to weigh in on the chocolate side of things. To complete a meal, I like clean simple flavors, ones that are refreshing and inspired by fruits. We Daulters are well known for having people over for dinner, and it seems that no matter what we decide to serve for dessert, our guests always leave saying, "Wow, that dessert was amazing."

Fall Pumpkin Spiced Cookies

We love to give cookies as gifts and, with our repurposing efforts around the house, we like to find various containers to reuse for gifting our cookies. The pumpkin cookies shown in the photo on the opposite page are in a repurposed fruit container. They are delicious and soft and a perfect fall treat. We love to eat them with a glass of rice milk.

1 cup whole wheat pastry flour

1 cup oat flour

1 teaspoon baking powder (recipe page 158)

½ teaspoon baking soda

½ teaspoon sea salt

½ teaspoon freshly grated nutmeg

1 teaspoon ground cinnamon

¼ teaspoon ground ginger

¼ teaspoon ground allspice

1 teaspoon vanilla extract

½ cup fresh or canned plain pumpkin purée

1 tablespoon unsalted butter

½ cup raw agave nectar

½ cup pure cane sugar

2 eggs

¼ cup coconut oil

confectioners' sugar, for dusting

Preheat oven to 350°F. Line a baking sheet with parchment paper.

In a large mixing bowl, blend together flours, baking powder, baking soda, salt, nutmeg, cinnamon, ginger, and allspice.

In a separate bowl, thoroughly mix vanilla, pumpkin purée, butter, agave nectar, and sugar. Add eggs, one at a time, then add oil and blend together until smooth.

Slowly add flour mixture to pumpkin mixture until you create a soft dough.

Roll out dough on a floured surface to about ¼ inch thick. Either use cookie cutters (perhaps a fall leaf), or drop into balls and flatten to ¼-inch-thick rounds on prepared baking sheet.

Bake for approximately 15 minutes, until light golden brown. They should be chewy on the inside. Sprinkle with confectioners' sugar right away and let cool. Serve with rice milk.

Makes 12–15 cookies

Growing Together:
Family Garden Plots

Children are more likely to try a wider variety of foods when they have a part in making them grow. Each of my kids (beginning around age two) has received his or her own special spot in the garden to grow up to two things of his or her choosing. They are responsible for tending to their patches and for harvesting the bounty later on. They have a great sense of pride in watching their foods grow and often turn it into a vegetable growing contest.

Delicious Gratitude Red Velvet Carrot Cupcakes

We had a gratitude birthday party for Lotus, and these cupcakes were on her list of what she wanted to serve her friends. The party was to let her friends know that she appreciates them and thinks about everything she is grateful for, as we honored her on her special day. You will love these!

Cook's Note: Although there are many natural food dyes on the market, and they are mostly made up of fruits and vegetables, the best thing to obtain a deep, rich, red velvet color is beet powder. (See resources section for where to buy.)

Cupcakes:
3 carrots, chopped
2½ cups whole wheat pastry flour
2 teaspoons wheat germ
1 teaspoon baking soda
1 cup pure cane sugar
1 tablespoon unsweetened cacao powder
1 cup coconut oil
2 eggs
½ cup buttermilk
1 teaspoon vanilla extract
1 teaspoon distilled white vinegar
⅓ cup beet powder

Frosting:
1 (8-ounce) package cream cheese, softened
½ cup pure cane sugar
1 tablespoon vanilla extract
1 tablespoon unsalted butter
1–2 drops mint extract (optional, to give frosting a light mint flavor)

Steam carrots until soft, about 8–10 minutes. In blender, purée carrots and set aside.

Preheat oven to 350°F. Line muffin pan with cupcake papers.

In a medium bowl, blend together flour, wheat germ, baking soda, sugar, and cacao powder.

In separate large mixing bowl, blend together oil, eggs, buttermilk, vanilla, carrot purée, and vinegar with a hand-held mixer. Add the dry ingredients to the wet and blend at a slow speed until well blended. Add beet powder and continue to mix with hand-held mixer until well blended. Spoon batter into cupcake papers a little less than halfway full.

Bake for about 20 minutes, until fork inserted into the center of a cupcake comes out clean. Let cool.

To make the frosting, in a mixing bowl, combine cream cheese with sugar and, with mixer, blend to a smooth consistency. Add vanilla, butter, and mint extract (if using), and continue to blend with the mixer until smooth. Frost cupcakes after they have cooled slightly. NOTE: I like to pipe my frosting through a bag with the tip cut off, so I can swirl the frosting on very easily, and it looks pretty, too!

Makes 15–18 cupcakes

Roasted Cinnamon Apple and Sweet Potato Galette

This dessert is so easy, yet it looks like a super-fancy treat. They say you eat with your eyes first, and this recipe is a beauty, and the great taste follows. This galette has a light and flaky crust, a sweet topping, and a little crunch from the almonds. I like to serve it after a light meal, as the sweet potatoes and apples are really filling. It is best to use a mandoline slicer to slice the sweet potato and apples. If you don't have one, slice them as thinly as possible.

1 sweet potato, thinly sliced

1–2 Gala apples, peeled and thinly sliced

1 teaspoon coconut oil

4 tablespoons honey

1 sheet puff pastry, chilled, not frozen

½ cup sliced almonds

1 teaspoon ground cinnamon, for dusting

whipped cream, for serving

Preheat oven to 350°F. Line a cookie sheet with parchment paper.

In a 9 x 13-inch baking dish, place sweet potato and apple slices, and drizzle with coconut oil and 1 tablespoon honey. Roast for approximately 15–18 minutes.

While sweet potato and apple slices are roasting, roll out puff pastry, ¼ inch thick, on a floured surface, into about a 12 x 20-inch rectangle. Create an edge on all sides by rolling up some pastry. Poke a fork in the center of the dough a couple of times. Move the dough to the parchment-lined cookie sheet.

Remove roasted sweet potato and apple slices from oven. Arrange slices all over dough, creating any pattern you like with them, and add sliced almonds on top. Keep the dough in one big piece. Drizzle with the rest of the honey and bake on the prepared cookie sheet for 15–18 minutes, until pastry has puffed up and is light and golden brown in color.

Sprinkle with a little cinnamon, let cool slightly, then cut into squares and serve with whipped cream.

Serves 8–10

Greening Together: Quick Tips!

Try the following:

- Turn off the water when you brush your teeth.

- Stop buying plastic water bottles and use a stainless steel one instead.

- Use canvas bags at the store (all stores, not just at the grocery).

- Turn off lights when not in the room.

- Use junk mail for art projects.

- Turn your old brown paper shopping bags into wrapping paper.

- Bike to work and consider having only one car per family.

- Only use cloth napkins.

- If you have a baby, try cloth diapers instead of disposables. (This practice helped our children naturally potty-train very early.)

Classic Gingerbread Cookies

The gingerbread man has a special status of sorts in our home. Whenever I suggest we make these cookies, the kids go crazy. They love to play with them, decorate them, and eventually get around to eating them. Lotus will take them to her wooden castle and play for hours. They inspire games like "bakery" and "school" and can be decorated with simple seeds, left plain, or topped with a little confectioners' sugar when ready to eat.

Cook's Note: You will need a gingerbread man cookie cutter.

3 cups whole wheat pastry flour

1 tablespoon baking powder (recipe page 158)

pinch sea salt

¼ teaspoon baking soda

½ teaspoon freshly grated nutmeg

1½ teaspoons ground cinnamon

1 teaspoon ground ginger

1 teaspoon ground allspice

1 tablespoon ground almonds

1 cup packed dark brown sugar

8 tablespoons (1 stick) unsalted butter, softened

2 eggs

½ cup water

½ cup blackstrap molasses

½ teaspoon vanilla extract

Preheat oven to 300°F. Line a cookie sheet with parchment paper.

In a large mixing bowl, blend together flour, baking powder, salt, baking soda, nutmeg, cinnamon, ginger, allspice, and ground almonds.

In a separate bowl, mix brown sugar and butter. Add eggs, water, molasses, and vanilla. Mix well. Add dry ingredients slowly until you create a slightly sticky dough.

Roll dough out on a lightly floured surface about ¼ inch thick. Use gingerbread man cookie cutters to shape your cookies. On prepared cookie sheet, line up your gingerbread cookies about an inch apart from one another.

Bake for 15–18 minutes, until light golden brown, so they will be chewy on the inside. Store in an airtight glass container for up to 1 week.

Makes 10–15 gingerbread cookies (depending on size of your cutter)

Dark Chocolate and Cinnamon Soup with Peppermint Agave Marshmallows

All kids like hot chocolate on a cold wintry day. My kids like to play "soup," where they create a soup, usually out of various tea blends, set the kids' table, and invite us all to eat. Of course, their favorite version of "soup" comes in the form of chocolate. This recipe, inspired by the creativity of child's play, is a really fun dessert twist on hot cocoa and marshmallows.

Cook's Note: Marshmallows must be left out overnight to harden, so be sure to make them at least a day before you need them.

Marshmallows:

½ cup water

3 tablespoons unflavored gelatin

2 cups raw agave nectar

¼ teaspoon sea salt

1 tablespoon vanilla extract

¼ teaspoon peppermint extract

Chocolate Soup:

¼ cup water

3 cups whole milk

½ cup raw agave nectar

3 tablespoons dark chocolate cacao powder

pinch ground cinnamon

½ cup heavy cream

To make the marshmallows, pour water in a bowl and pour gelatin over the top. Let it sit for about 5–7 minutes while the gelatin blooms.

Oil a 9 x 13-inch baking dish.

In a saucepan over medium heat, mix together agave nectar and salt. Let it get warm, but do not bring to a boil.

Add agave mixture to dissolved gelatin and transfer to a mixing bowl. Add vanilla and peppermint extracts. With the whisk attachment, whisk for about 10 minutes, until mixture has essentially doubled in size and is a fluffy, sticky goo. Pour into oiled dish and leave out to harden overnight. Then, cut into squares of your desired size. Depending on how small you cut them, you can make up to 50 marshmallows.

To make the chocolate soup, in a saucepan, on high heat, bring water to a boil.

Turn heat down to medium and add milk, agave nectar, cacao powder, cinnamon, and heavy cream. Stir until well blended, about 2 minutes.

Serve soup warm in your favorite bowl with a straw and spoon, topped with the marshmallows. Yum!

Serves 4–6 (with leftover marshmallows)

Growing Together:
Flower Faeries

Lotus loves going on "flower faerie hunts" with her friends. They gather sticks, flowers, and seeds in a basket and then use those natural elements to decorate their faerie houses. Lotus even has a faerie living in her part of the garden. Growing flowers among the vegetables in our garden gives her the freedom to adorn her faerie house and our dinner table with her beautiful arrangements. She also loves to collect rose petals for her bath, just like her mom!

Cooking Together:
Sweeten It Up

Desserts are meant to be sweet. It's important, however, to manage the sugar intake of our children and to know that there are some decent choices for replacing the refined sugar in almost any recipe. When talking about sugar with your children, help them to see how sugar can affect their bodies and moods, so they better understand the benefit of what I call "nature's candy" (fruit).

Here is a brief primer on some alternatives to refined sugar when making homemade sweets:

Raw Agave Nectar: Agave nectar looks like a thin version of honey and has a low glycemic index, so it does not induce mood swings. It is naturally high in antioxidants. When the agave nectar is raw, it has been minimally processed, which keeps the fructose levels down and closer to their natural state.

Coconut Sugar: Coconut sugar comes from coconut palm sugar blossoms and also has a low glycemic index. It's typically organic, usually unprocessed, unfiltered, and unbleached. It's available online and at most natural health food stores.

Local Honey: I love honey because it's natural, often local, and has many medicinal properties. If you can find a local harvester for honey, that's a great option, because eating local honey can help with allergies and boost your immune system.

Organic Pure Cane Sugar: This sugar has a sort of molasses taste and has not been super-processed. This is a good baking sugar.

Fruit: I regularly use fruit to sweeten various recipes, including frozen treats. When you buy fruit that is in season, you have the best chance of catching it at its sweetest moment!

Zoë's Banana Scallops with Cinnamon-Sugar Chips and Mint-Agave Whipped Cream

Zoë and I love the show Top Chef. He saw one of the chefs make a dish he called banana scallops, and Zoë thought it was so cool, he wanted to create his own signature dish. It's simple, but I was inspired by his creativity. So this dish is all his. Nicely done, sweetie! (By the way, he also styled this picture himself. Not bad for a 13-year-old boy, right?)

Mint-Agave Whipped Cream:

1 cup heavy whipping cream

¼ cup raw agave nectar

1–2 drops mint extract

Cinnamon-Sugar Chips:

5 flour tortillas

¼ cup coconut oil

¼ cup cinnamon-sugar mixture

Banana Scallops:

1 pat unsalted butter

2 firm bananas, thinly sliced (use a mandoline if you can)

¼ cup pure cane sugar

To make the whipped cream, pour whipping cream into bowl of an electric mixer and mix on medium speed. Add agave nectar and mint extract drops. Mix for 4–5 minutes, until it becomes frothy. Taste for sweetness and add more agave nectar or mint flavoring if you want. Refrigerate until ready to serve.

Make the chips next, so they will be ready exactly when the bananas are done. Preheat oven to 350°F. Brush each tortilla with oil, and then sprinkle with a little cinnamon-sugar mixture. Bake for about 8 minutes, until crisp.

To cook the bananas, in a large skillet, melt butter and place bananas, in a single layer, in the pan. Sprinkle a little sugar on top of each one. Cook until browned, about 3–4 minutes, then flip over and cook second side until browned.

Serve warm banana slices on top of a cinnamon-sugar chip and with some mint-agave whipped cream on the side.

Serves 4

Chocolate Chip Cookies

Most people know and love the classic flavor of chocolate chip cookies and milk. I can still remember the smell of the house when I would come home after school, and my mom would have cookies and milk waiting for my sister and me. This version, with its dark chocolate chips adding a natural antioxidant, and its boost of wheat germ, is a little healthier than the traditional version, but still a tasty classic.

1¼ cups whole wheat pastry flour

1 cup quinoa flour

1 teaspoon baking soda

½ teaspoon hemp seed powder (use your coffee grinder)

1 teaspoon wheat germ

¼ teaspoon sea salt

1 cup raw agave nectar

¼ cup packed brown sugar

3 tablespoons unsalted butter, softened

2 eggs

1 teaspoon vanilla extract

1½ cups dark chocolate chips

Preheat oven to 350°F. Line a cookie sheet with parchment paper.

In a large mixing bowl, blend together flours, baking soda, hemp seed powder, wheat germ, and salt.

In a separate bowl, mix agave nectar, brown sugar, butter, eggs, and vanilla. Stir in chocolate chips.

Slowly add the flour mixture to the wet ingredients until you create a batter.

On prepared cookie sheet, place cookie batter in balls that measure about 1 tablespoon. Cookies should be about 2 inches apart. Do not press down.

Cook for approximately 8–10 minutes, until light golden brown around the edges.

Makes 20–25 cookies

Greening Together:
What We Eat Out Of!

I think it's important to choose plastic alternatives for dishware and reusable products for packing lunches, whenever possible. I think it's aesthetically more beautiful, which creates a nicer eating environment for your children, AND it's better for Mother Earth. Single-use plastic bags are used on the average for about 20 minutes, but they can take hundreds of years to degrade — whether it is in a landfill, a tree, or one of our poor suffering oceans. Recycling is largely a myth, as less than 5% of all plastics are currently recycled. My friend Jay owns a business called Life Without Plastic. Can you even imagine our lives without any plastic? For great plastic alternatives, check this out: http://lifewithoutplastic.com/.

Simple Peach Berry Soufflés

Have you ever seen a recipe or picture of beautifully styled food and just thought it was out of your league? Well, that has always been my reaction to soufflés! Ever intimidated by gorgeous soufflé photos, I forced myself to try to make one. They are not as hard as you might think.

Cook's Note: You will need ramekins to make this properly.

¼ **cup raspberry jam**
1 cup fresh raspberries, blueberries, or blackberries (whatever you prefer)
1 fresh peach, cut into small pieces
zest and juice of 1 lemon
1 cup whole milk
1 tablespoon arrowroot
1 cup raw agave nectar, divided
3 large eggs, separated
1 tablespoon unsalted butter
confectioners' sugar, for topping (optional)

Preheat oven to 400°F. Coat 6 ramekins with butter.

Place about a tablespoon of raspberry jam, a few berries, and a few small peach pieces into each ramekin.

In a saucepan over medium heat, combine lemon zest and juice, milk, arrowroot, ½ cup agave nectar, and egg yolks. Bring to a boil. Whisk constantly until a pudding consistency forms, then whisk in butter. Transfer to a mixing bowl.

In a separate bowl, with a hand-held mixer, beat egg whites until soft peaks form. Add remaining ½ cup agave nectar. Fold whites into pudding mixture, and blend together with a fork.

Spoon some of the mixture over the top of each ramekin. Bake for about 15 minutes, until they puff up and are lightly golden. Remove, sift confectioners' sugar over the tops, and serve warm.

Serves 6

Cooking Together:
Invite Someone Special to Dinner

Ask your children to create a special invitation for dinner to give to a teacher, neighbor, or new friend. We always have our children's teachers over for dinner when the school year starts, which helps the teacher get a more intimate glimpse of our home life and helps our children feel more connected to their teachers. The kids are always excited and proud to feed their teachers and find many ways to make the evening special. When we break bread with others, we share more than food — we share connection, friendship, and nourishment.

Flourless Chocolate Cake (Gluten-Free)

My friend Ashley does not eat gluten, so this cake recipe is dedicated to her. Folks with gluten intolerance basically cannot have products containing a certain type of protein found in things like wheat, barley, oats, and rye. The rich dark chocolate of this cake is moist and delicious. This recipe is fantastic served with coffee ice cream.

1 (4-ounce) bar dark chocolate with cacao, broken into pieces

8 tablespoons (1 stick) unsalted butter

½ cup pure cane sugar

1 teaspoon vanilla extract

2 eggs

½ cup honey

¼ cup unsweetened cacao powder, sifted, plus more to serve

Preheat the oven to 375°F. Lightly oil a 9½-inch round cake pan.

On the stove, boil water in a pot. As soon as water boils, turn down to medium-high heat and place a stainless steel bowl on top of the water. Melt chocolate and butter together in the bowl. Do not let the bottom of the bowl touch the water. This process will take about 5–7 minutes. Stir frequently, so the chocolate does not burn.

In a separate large mixing bowl, combine sugar and vanilla. Mix melted chocolate mixture into sugar mixture, and with a wooden spoon, stir until well blended.

Add eggs, one at a time, and then honey. Stir until well blended. Sift in cacao powder and stir to combine. Pour batter into cake pan. Bake for 20–25 minutes.

Let cool slightly and serve warm with cacao powder sifted on top and a side of coffee ice cream.

Serves 8

Triple Berry Cream Cheese Tarts

I like fruit-inspired desserts, and I love making these tarts. They are very charming, baked in their mini cast-iron skillets, and absolutely delicious! These pans are available online at Lodge Cast Iron Company. If you do not have them, you can use a jumbo muffin pan (which, like these mini skillets, has 4-inch-diameter muffin cups).

1 cup cream cheese, softened

½ cup raw agave nectar

1 sheet puff pastry, chilled, not frozen

unsalted butter, approximately ½ teaspoon per mini pan or muffin cup

¼ cup raspberry jam

½ cup fresh blackberries

¼ cup fresh blueberries

poppy seeds and sesame seeds, for topping

Preheat oven to 400°F. When it reaches full temperature, place empty cast-iron pans or muffin pan in the oven for 8–10 minutes to preheat. (This recipe makes 8–10 tarts, so if you don't have that many skillets, you'll need to make this recipe in several batches.)

In a mixer, combine cream cheese and agave nectar until well whipped.

On a lightly floured surface, roll out puff pastry to about ¼ inch thick. Using a round cookie cutter, cut out 4-inch-wide circles of dough. The circles should be sized to lie perfectly in the bottom of each pan or muffin cup.

Pull hot pans out of the oven and decrease the oven temperature to 350°F. Place a small dollop of butter in each pan or muffin cup to coat the bottom of each, and add a dough round in each pan or muffin cup. Poke the top of each dough round with a fork only once (this will help them rise a bit).

Add a spoonful of cream cheese mixture to each dough round, and then add a spoonful of raspberry jam. Add a couple of blackberries and a couple of blueberries to the top of each tart, and then sprinkle each with poppy and sesame seeds.

Bake for 15–18 minutes, until lightly browned and puffed up a bit. Serve warm.

Makes 8–10 tarts

Greening Together:
Make Nature Toys

Instead of buying new toys for your children, consider nature as your toy store. Here are some ideas that we have used with our kids.

For winter solstice last year, Zoë found a big tree branch that had already been cut down, and he and my husband cut and sanded many pieces to make blocks for Bodhi. Zoë also treated them with natural orange-scented Stockmar polish. They smell great, and Bodhi loves them.

Go on a nature walk and gather pinecones, sticks, walnuts, and leaves and put them in separate baskets for your kids to play with. Make sure the pinecones aren't sticky with resin before bringing them into your home.

Take seeds from a pumpkin, wash and dry them, paint them with watercolor paint, and string them into necklaces.

Dana's Raw Vegan Apple Pie

My friend Dana makes a wonderful raw apple pie, and she was kind enough to share it with me for this book. Everyone digs into this hearty pie and loves its fresh flavors and crunch. A big hug to Dana for sharing her love-filled raw apple pie with the world — this is a real treat!

3 cups raw almonds
1½ cups pitted dates
6–8 Fuji apples, cored
3 tablespoons raw agave nectar
1½ teaspoons ground cinnamon
4½ teaspoons ground flax seed
4½ teaspoons fresh-squeezed lemon juice
¾ cup raisins

Grind almonds in a food processor or coffee grinder and add dates, a few at a time, to taste. Press the mixture evenly into the bottom and sides of a 9-inch pie pan. Set aside and make the filling.

Using a mandoline slicer, thinly slice apples. Put apple slices into a large mixing bowl and add agave nectar, cinnamon, flax seed, lemon juice, and raisins. Mix well.

Place apple mixture into the piecrust and serve within a day.

Serves 10

Greening Together:
Make Homemade Gifts

Zoë gets invited to a lot of birthday parties, and because we value handmade items, he knows that if he wants to go to the party he has to make the gift. We buy any art supplies, but he needs to create the final gift. He developed a hand-sewn monster-type of doll that he makes from old clothes that we put into our fabric bin, gives them all unique names, and now his friends are dying to get theirs. He started an eco-gifting trend, and other kids in his class at school are now making homemade gifts. Being green can be trendy, too!

Chewy Decadent Caramels

These candies are seriously good! They are candy, so we don't make them very often, but when we do, they're always a huge hit. We usually make them for folks at our children's Waldorf School, and our maintenance executive, RJ, is always first in line for these treats.

Cook's Note: Make these caramels when you have a lot of energy, as you have to stir for a long while. This might be an opportunity for you to "pass the spoon," so to speak, to any older children whom you are teaching how to cook. I would allow Zoë (who is 13) to try this, for example.

2 cups heavy whipping cream
2 cups pure cane sugar
¾ cup raw agave nectar
8 tablespoons (1 stick) unsalted butter
pinch sea salt

Butter a medium-sized (4 x 7-inch) ceramic dish. Set aside.

Combine all ingredients in a heavy-bottomed saucepan over high heat. Bring all ingredients to a boil, then turn down to medium heat and stir and stir and stir. . . . Don't stop stirring or it will burn! Continue stirring for about 40 minutes!

The mixture will get thick and gooey. Remember to keep stirring so it does not ever boil in big bubbles. It will be hot and may gently boil, but do not leave unattended.

It is done when it is a thick consistency and medium-brown in color. Pour into the buttered ceramic dish. It will start to harden up almost immediately.

Let cool before cutting. I wrap each candy individually in white parchment paper or waxed paper, especially if I'm giving them as a gift.

Makes 40–45 pieces (depending upon how small you cut pieces)

Homespun Extras

Many folks don't think to make their own condiments, but these "extras" are easy to make and far more healthful than commercial versions. Make these homespun extras yourself and you can be confident that every ingredient that goes into them is of the quality you desire.

Lotus Loves Honey Butter

Honey butter is an easy-to-prepare spread to sweeten up a large variety of foods. Lotus is our resident honey butter maker, and we use it on breads, toast, quinoa, crackers, and even spiced cakes. It's really delicious.

8 tablespoons (1 stick) unsalted butter, softened
⅓ cup honey

Mix butter and honey together until nicely whipped and smooth. Use immediately, or store in the refrigerator for up to 1 week.

Serves 6

Simple Herbed Butter

Herbed butter is great for roasted corn, baked potatoes, and roasted veggies. It's another very simple recipe that can have many variations according to what you have growing in your garden or your personal flavor preferences.

Cook's Note: Other great variations are pepper-dill and garlic-chive.

8 tablespoons (1 stick) butter, softened
finely chopped fresh basil leaves
finely chopped fresh thyme leaves
pinch sea salt and black pepper

Mix butter, basil, thyme, salt, and pepper together until nicely whipped and smooth. Taste and add more seasoning as desired. Refrigerate until ready to use.

Serves 6

Fresh Fig Jam

Figs go well with both sweet and savory foods. The trick to this recipe is using fresh figs, because they are the sweetest and purest form of fig essence. Delicious!

4 pounds fresh figs, washed, stemmed, and cut into pieces
1 cup honey
1 cup raw agave nectar
½ cup chopped walnuts, ground into a powder (use your coffee grinder)
juice and zest of 1 lemon

In a large saucepan, mix together figs, honey, agave nectar, walnut powder, and lemon juice and zest. Simmer over medium heat, stirring constantly, for about 20 minutes.

Cover and let sit on low heat for another 10 minutes. Uncover and stir until jam thickens, another 10–15 minutes. Store in airtight glass jars in the refrigerator for up to 3 weeks.

Makes 2 jars

Scrumptious Strawberry Agave Syrup

This syrup is great on pancakes, waffles, or even ice cream. What I love about this recipe is that you can make it with any berry you prefer. Strawberries and blueberries are my favorite.

2 cups chopped fresh strawberries
1 cup raw agave nectar
juice and zest of ½ lemon

In a large saucepan, mix together strawberries, agave nectar, and lemon juice and zest.

Simmer on medium heat, stirring constantly, for about 15 minutes.

Pour into a blender and blend to a smooth consistency. Use warm or cold. Can be stored in an airtight glass jar in the refrigerator for up to 2 weeks.

Makes 2 cups

Cooking Together: Love Delivers

My local community has great businesses that will deliver organic produce to your front door. As a busy mom who has a lot of mouths to feed, it's great to have this option. My favorite is L.O.V.E. Delivery! First, who doesn't want to get a little love delivered to their front door? Second, the company has amazing delicious produce and always gives a fresh flower. Check your local area for organic produce delivery services as an option for fresh convenience, and another way to support your local farmers.

Mustard

I love making mustard because I can create all sorts of variations to use as amazing additions to meats, dips, and sandwiches. The kids use mustard seeds to play with or press into dough ornaments. Be sure to begin making mustard the night before you need it; some parts of the recipe need to refrigerate overnight.

Cook's Note: Add a pinch of horseradish to spice it up if you want!

2 tablespoons dry mustard
2 eggs
1 cup white wine vinegar
½ cup yellow mustard seeds
½ cup brown mustard seeds
½ cup water
¼ cup honey (add more if you need it a little sweeter)
¼ teaspoon sea salt
¼ teaspoon black pepper

In a large saucepan, bring dry mustard, eggs, and vinegar to a boil. Let simmer until thick. Store in refrigerator overnight.

In a separate bowl, combine yellow and brown mustard seeds with water. Let sit overnight.

Next day, combine the two mixtures in a blender. Purée to a silky consistency, adding honey and salt and pepper to taste.

Store in an airtight glass jar in the refrigerator for up to 4 weeks.

Makes 4 cups

Tomato Catsup

Most everyone in our house loves catsup, and this is a fun recipe that can be made, stored, or even given away as gifts. Lotus is our real catsup connoisseur, so if it passes her test, you know it's a great recipe.

8 medium-size, ripe tomatoes, cut in big pieces
1½ yellow onions, diced
5 garlic cloves, minced
2 teaspoons ground coriander seeds
¼ cup raw agave nectar
¼ cup dark brown sugar
juice and zest of ½ lemon
¼ cup red wine vinegar
1 teaspoon sea salt
¼ teaspoon ground cinnamon
¼ teaspoon ground cloves
¼ teaspoon ground cumin
1 tablespoon ground pistachios (use your coffee grinder)

In a large saucepan, mix together all ingredients. Let simmer on medium heat until thick, about 10–12 minutes. Stir occasionally and watch that it does not burn.

Pour all ingredients in a blender and purée to a smooth consistency. Store in an airtight glass jar in the refrigerator for up to 4 weeks.

Makes 4 cups

Tofu Mayo

Until I became interested in making my own condiments, I didn't really know what mayonnaise was. I had never really liked it, and in fact, for some reason, it was one of the foods I was always afraid of as a kid. Now that I make my own, I enjoy a classic BLT every so often.

1 egg yolk
½ cup soft tofu
1 tablespoon white wine vinegar
juice of ½ lemon
¼ teaspoon dry mustard
2 pinches sea salt
2 pinches black pepper
1 cup canola oil

In a blender, mix together egg yolk, tofu, vinegar, lemon juice, dry mustard, salt, and pepper. Pulse a couple of times. Slowly pour in oil as you mix on low until well blended.

Chill before serving. Can be stored in an airtight glass jar in the refrigerator for up to 4 weeks.

Makes approximately 4 cups

Dill Dip

Dill dip is so refreshing that it makes a great dip for vegetables and fritters. It is also a great sauce for a veggie burger or even sweet potato fries.

1 cup sour cream
1 cup homemade mayonnaise (recipe page 156)
¼ teaspoon garlic powder
1 tablespoon dried dill weed
1 tablespoon minced fresh parsley
¼ teaspoon sea salt

In a medium-sized bowl, mix all ingredients together. Chill before serving. Can be stored in the refrigerator in an airtight glass jar for about 1 week.

Makes 2 cups

Everyday Garden Salsa

Everybody loves salsa! It's refreshing, fun, and a great party dish. Why not grab some fresh ingredients from your garden and whip up an easy version of an everyday classic. My friend's Mexican grandmother taught me this recipe, and everybody loves it. The secret to this recipe . . . the limes!

1 cup chopped grape or cherry tomatoes
1 large, juicy tomato, chopped into small pieces (about 1 cup)
½ cup chopped cilantro
½ yellow onion, finely chopped (about ½ cup)
1 teaspoon sea salt
1 teaspoon freshly ground pepper
½ teaspoon garlic powder
juice of 3 limes

In a large bowl, combine tomatoes, cilantro, onion, salt, pepper, and garlic powder. Gently mix in the lime juice. Serve immediately or chill in an airtight container and serve when ready. Lasts for about 4 days.

Serves 4

Strawberry-Mango Salsa

Have some fun with a summer salsa. This is a combination sweet and savory version of salsa that the kids love, and it is always a hit at parties!

1 cup chopped strawberries
1 whole mango, chopped into small pieces
½ cup chopped cilantro
½ yellow onion, chopped finely
1 teaspoon sea salt
juice of 1 lime
juice of ½ lemon

In a large bowl, combine strawberries, mango, cilantro, onion, and salt. Gently mix in the lime and lemon juice. Serve immediately or chill in an airtight container and serve when ready. Lasts for about 4 days.

Serves 4

Aluminum-Free Baking Powder

Many companies add aluminum to their baking powder, and nobody needs that! There are several brands you can buy that do not contain aluminum, but you have to read the labels. When baking, it's always important to use fresh baking powder to ensure that your baked goods will rise properly. Making your own baking powder will allow you to always have fresh aluminum-free baking powder in the house.

1 part baking soda
2 parts cream of tartar
1 part arrowroot
½ part hemp seed, ground in coffee grinder

In a medium-size bowl, mix all ingredients together. Store in an airtight jar for up to 2 months.

Table of Equivalents

Some of the conversions in these lists have been slightly rounded for measuring convenience.

VOLUME

U.S.	metric
¼ teaspoon	1.25 milliliters
½ teaspoon	2.5 milliliters
¾ teaspoon	3.75 milliliters
1 teaspoon	5 milliliters
1 tablespoon (3 teaspoons)	15 milliliters
2 tablespoons	30 milliliters
3 tablespoons	45 milliliters
1 fluid ounce (2 tablespoons)	30 milliliters
¼ cup (4 tablespoons)	60 milliliters
⅓ cup	80 milliliters
½ cup	120 milliliters
⅔ cup	160 milliliters
1 cup	240 milliliters
2 cups (1 pint)	480 milliliters
4 cups (1 quart or 32 ounces)	960 milliliters
1 gallon (4 quarts)	3.8 liters

WEIGHT:

U.S.	metric
1 ounce (by weight)	28 grams
1 pound	448 grams
2.2 pounds	1 kilogram

LENGTH:

U.S.	metric
⅛ inch	3 millimeters
¼ inch	6 millimeters
½ inch	12 millimeters
1 inch	2.5 centimeters

OVEN TEMPERATURE:

Fahrenheit	Celsius
250	120
275	140
300	150
325	160
350	180
375	190
400	200
425	220
450	230
475	240
500	260

Resources

Anni's Books and Web Sites

Ice Pop Joy (50 healthy, tasty organic ice pops for families)
www.icepopjoy.com

Organically Raised: Conscious Cooking for Babies and Toddlers
www.organicallyraisedcookbook.com

Bamboo: Conscious Family Living Magazine
www.bamboofamilymag.com

Food + Life Styling:
www.deliciousgratitude.com

Photographer
Alexandra DeFurio
www.defuriophotography.com

Green & Organic Experts
Alan Greene, MD
(Pediatrician & Author of *Raising Baby Green* & *Feeding Baby Green*)
www.drgreene.com

Healthy Child Healthy World
www.healthychild.org

Lauren Feder, MD
(Naturopath for children's ailments)
www.drfeder.com

Organic Authority
www.organicauthority.com

Gardening, Farms, Delivery, & Markets
Compost Bins
www.naturemill.com

Local Harvest
(to locate your local farmers' market)
www.localharvest.org

L.O.V.E. Food Delivery
(Organic; greater Los Angeles)
www.lovedelivery.com

MinifarmBox (Conor's place)
www.minifarmbox.com

Pick-your-own farms
www.pickyourown.org

Greening Information
Eco-bags
www.ecobags.com

Freecycle
www.freecycle.org

Planet Green
www.planetgreen.discovery.com

Re-Use-It
www.reuseit.com

Treehugger
www.treehugger.com

Cookware and Container Products
"Green" cookware
www.green-pan.com

GreenPots
(These are my absolute faves!)
www.greencookingpots.com

Hipcooks
(They make these amazing round cutting boards! I LOVE mine.)
www.hipcooks.com

Klean Kanteen
www.kleankanteen.com

Life Without Plastic
(My friend Jay's amazing store — you can buy Santus Mundo there.)
www.lifewithoutplastic.com

Lodge Cast Iron Cookware
www.lodgemfg.com

Tabletops Unlimited
www.tabletopsunltd.com

World Kitchen
www.shopworldkitchen.com

Specialty Food Items
Beet Powder
www.znaturalfoods.com/Beet-Root-
    Powder-Organic-(1-lb)

Born Free Eggs (If you don't have access to
local eggs, these are great eggs.)
www.bornfreeeggs.com

Braggs Amino Acids
www.bragg.com/products/la.html

Dagoba Chocolate
www.dagobachocolate.com

Equal Exchange (amazing chocolate)
www.equalexchange.coop

Fair Haven (great flours)
www.fairhavenflour.com

King Arthur Flour
(love their all-purpose flour)
www.kingarthurflour.com/shop/items/
    king-arthur-organic-all-purpose-flour-5-lb

Madhava Raw Agave Nectar
www.madhavahoney.com/
    AgaveNectar.aspx

Hemp Seeds & Other Super Grains
www.navitasnaturals.com

Natural Food Colors
www.naturesflavors.com

Organic Coconut Sugar
www.bigtreefarms.com/
    sweettreecoconutsugar

Organic & Natural Sweeteners
Wholesome Sweeteners
www.wholesomesweeteners.com

Anni's Favorite Family Blogs
City Mommy
www.citymommy.com

Farm Mama
(Sara is just down right inspiring!)
farmama.typepad.com

Green Moms
www.greenmoms.com

Holistic Moms Network
www.holisticmoms.org

Hot Moms Club
www.hotmomsclub.com

Mocha Moms
www.mochamoms.org

Small Things Blog with Ginny Sheller
(Amazing Mama to six kids!)
www.gsheller.com

Anni's Favorite Family Magazines
Bamboo ~ Conscious Family Living
www.bamboofamilymag.com

KIWI Magazine
www.kiwimagonline.com

Mindful Mama
www.mindful-mama.com

Mothering Magazine
www.mothering.com

Rhythm of The Home
www.rhythmofthehome.com

Pure Style Living with Anna Getty
www.purestyleliving.com

Acknowledgments

A Big Hug & Acknowledgments to:

I want to thank so many people who worked to make this book happen and helped turn my vision into a reality. Tim, my loving husband who is my champion and who took complete care of me and our children while I was writing like a maniac (especially that last weekend before Solstice!). To Zoe, Lotus, Bodhi & River, who are at most photo shoots and who now food design what they eat and even play "photo shoot." Thank you for your patience, cuteness, and little laughs. To my mom for her endless love and support, I love you, and my in-laws, Bonnie & Dan, for your generous support and care.

Alexandra…I adore you and am so grateful to have the best and most creative photographer on my team. You are inspirational, a great friend, good mama, and overall super rad chick!

Amy Brawley! Mama we would not have been able to do this book without you. All those photo shoots, with us passing River back and forth, holding him on our hips, while positioning the bounce and trying to create food magic, were incredibly challenging, but SUPER fun! You are awesome and I cannot thank you enough.

Thank you to my amazing editor, Megan Hiller, at Sellers. Your eye for detail is incredible and your support is priceless. I have loved working on these projects with you and I appreciate your vision. Thank you to the art/design department at Sellers and for listening to my input.

Anna Getty, my friend and co-cheerleader for the organic movement, your work inspires me and I am so glad we are in this together.

Dr. Greene, thank you for your vision and time and commitment to healthy children and a healthy planet.

Thank you, dear mama friends, for all the love and support and help with the kids. Our community is amazing! Kelly, Nicki, Cindy, Amy, Ashley, Anny, Sabine, Melanie, Luann, Dana, and Tnah…you women seriously rock and are all gorgeous!

Thank you, Alexander Gordin, for hanging out and making banana bread. We love you and Max Daulter. Thank you, Eva and Maya, for taking some pictures with Lotus.

Thank you, Meredith, another project to be proud of.

Sandra and your girls, thank you for helping me clean up when I was exhausted!

Thank you to Highland Hall Waldorf School for allowing me to use your beautiful campus for photo shoots.

Thank you to my friend Jay at Life Without Plastic for supplying me with the best goods!

Thank you to my friend, Mark Kelly, at Lodge Cast Iron! LOVE your stuff.

Thank you NOVA Natural! Ted and the crew are amazing and your natural kids' toys are beautiful and special. I adore you guys!

Roberta at World of Green & Aaron at Olive & Myrtle! Your consciousness around sustainability and great green products is inspiring.

Entertaining Elephants & Cranky Pants, thank you for the clothes for photo shoots! Amazingly cute.

Greenpots, Cookware, Tabletops Unlimited, World Kitchen, Kuhn Rikon, Bake it Pretty, and Soolip for your amazing products that helped turn this book into a beautiful classic for families.

Index